A CLASSICAL APPROACH TO JAZZ PIANO

EXPLORING HARMONY

DOMINIC ALLDIS

For more information about Dominic Alldis, visit his website at

www.canzona.demon.co.uk

ISBN 0-634-00177-9

HAL•LEONARD®
CORPORATION

7777 W. BLUEMOUND RD. P.O. BOX 13819 MILWAUKEE, WI 53213

Visit Hal Leonard Online at
www.halleonard.com

PREFACE

When I was thirteen years old, I was invited to play the piano in the school jazz band under the auspices of our young and enthusiastic Director of Music. This involved performing hundreds of Dixieland and blues arrangements in numerous settings; school concerts, church halls and even the occasional pub! Following this early yet invaluable experience, I was on my own musically speaking, learning jazz piano by transcribing solos from records, picking up chord progressions and "licks" from more senior jazz musicians or else working things out by myself. Jazz education has come a long way since those days; there is now a comprehensive catalogue of tutor books, transcriptions and play-along records for the aspiring jazz pianist, many of which are thoroughly researched and well presented. However, there is a lack of clearly written tutor books aimed at the classical pianist seeking a concise and coherent introduction to jazz piano.

Since I come from an ostensibly classical music background, it seemed an obvious challenge to try and consolidate my knowledge and playing experience into a distinctly *classical* method, one that would appeal to pianists from a similar musical background to my own. With this in mind, I have tried to write in a language that will be immediately comprehensible to classical pianists. This first book deals with harmony, providing the knowledge required to make arrangements of songs using chord symbol notation.

The book is divided into two sections:

Section One concerns basic harmony, beginning with a preparatory chapter on scales, intervals and triads. It is followed by chapters on jazz chords, three-part harmony, accompaniment styles and basic jazz theory.

Section Two is a study of advanced harmony, beginning with reharmonisation. It is followed by chapters on four and five-part harmony, upper-structure triads, block chords, pentatonic harmony and the influence of classical piano music on jazz.

Finally, this book represents the culmination of hundreds of hours spent teaching jazz piano. It should be an enjoyable course of study for anyone who loves jazz piano and wants to make steps towards understanding the vast array of harmonic possibilities open to the improvising pianist. It also offers more advanced jazz pianists a process that should engender a more refined and consistent harmonic approach, as well as providing an insight into the advanced harmonic concepts employed by the world's finest jazz pianists.

Dominic Alldis is a professor of jazz piano at the Royal Academy of Music and gives classes in classical harmony, composition and improvisation at the Junior Department of the Royal College of Music in London. He is also active on the jazz scene both as a pianist and a singer, leading his own quartet and writing for various ensembles. He has released several albums, including *Turn Out The Stars* featuring songs written by the legendary jazz pianist Bill Evans. Information about his recordings and performing activities can be found on his web page: www.canzona.demon.co.uk.

A CLASSICAL APPROACH

TO

JAZZ PIANO

(Harmony)

Contents:

PART ONE

Contents

PART ONE

A theory of jazz harmony has gradually evolved alongside the performers, composers, arrangers and teachers who have contributed significantly to the development of jazz music. In **Part One,** we shall learn about the rudiments of jazz harmony and how to make simple but effective arrangements of standard songs on the piano. It will include chapters on: **preparation, jazz chords, three-part harmony, accompaniment models, playing the melody** and **basic jazz theory**.

CHAPTER ONE

PREPARATION

Since jazz theory has developed fairly recently, there are a number of musical terms and notation systems in use, most of which can easily be deciphered. We shall begin with a review the basic theory, including **major** and **minor scales**, **intervals**, **triads**, **inverted triads** and **chord symbols**, and identify discrepancies between jazz and classical terminology.

SCALES

Western classical music is based on **diatonic scales**. They consist of rows of notes in various sequences of steps and half steps. In jazz, there are five essential scales:

a) the **major** scale
b) the **melodic minor** scale
c) the **harmonic minor** scale
d) the **natural minor** scale
e) the **dorian minor** scale

In the key of C, they are as follows:

a) The **major** scale:

Figure 1-1

The **C major scale** is unique in comprising a sequence of steps and half steps that coincide with the white keys on the keyboard. The intervallic order (the sequence of steps and half steps) for all major scales is as follows:

step - step - half step - step - step - step - half step

b) The **melodic minor** scale:

Figure 1-2

In classical theory, the melodic minor scale is a composite of two scales:

i) **ascending** it is the same as the major scale but with a *minor* third.

ii) **descending** it is the same as the *natural minor* scale.

The term *melodic* minor refers to the way melodies are conventionally composed in classical music when written in a minor key. In jazz theory, the term *melodic minor scale* is generally applied to only the *ascending* portion of the scale (as shown above). The intervallic order for all melodic minor scales in jazz is as follows:

step - half step - step - step - step - step - half step

c) The **harmonic minor** scale:

Figure 1-3

The **C harmonic minor scale** is the same as the melodic minor scale shown above except for the sixth degree, which is played as a *minor* sixth (flattened sixth), creating an augmented second between the sixth and seventh degree of the scale. The intervallic order for all harmonic minor scales is as follows:

step - haif step - step - step - half step - augmented second - half step

d) The **natural minor** scale:

Figure 1-4

The **C natural minor scale** consists of the same notes as the major scale an interval of a minor third above. In this example, C natural minor contains the same notes as E♭ major. They also share the same key signature (three flats). C minor is referred to as the *relative minor scale* of E♭ major, whereas E♭ major is referred to as the *relative major scale* of C minor. The natural minor scale contains a minor third, minor sixth and minor seventh (flattened sixth and seventh). The intervallic order for all natural minor scales is as follows:

step - half step - step - step - half step - step - step

e) The **dorian minor** scale:

Figure 1-5

The **C dorian minor scale** consists of the same notes as the melodic minor scale but with a minor seventh. The scale contains a minor third, major sixth and minor seventh (flattened seventh). The intervallic order for all dorian minor scales is as follows:

step - half step - step - step - step - half step - step

Please note the following:

• The above scales can be transposed into all twelve keys.

• If you have previously studied classical piano or any other classical instrument, much of this information will already have been assimilated while practising scales and arpeggios, and from playing pieces written in major and minor keys. Though it is not essential to be able to play all major and minor scales perfectly to begin playing jazz, it will be invaluable to spend some time reviewing these scales so that they can be found easily in all twelve keys.

• You may wish to purchase a *scale manual* containing major and minor scales and arpeggios, available from any good music shop.

INTERVALS

We can express this distance between any two notes in the following ways:

a) As the sum total of steps and half steps (the distance between C and F is two steps and one half step).

b) As an **interval**. Since jazz, like classical music, is based on diatonic scales (major and minor scales), it makes sense to refer to these scales when describing the distance between two notes.

The intervals found within an octave are shown below, in this case between two Cs, followed by their description using jazz terminology:

Figure 1-6

Key:

a) minor second (half step or semitone)
b) major second (step or tone)
c) minor third
d) major third
e) perfect fourth
f) augmented fourth or diminished fifth (tristep or tritone)
g) perfect fifth
h) augmented fifth or minor sixth
i) major sixth
j) augmented sixth or minor seventh
k) major seventh
l) octave

Exercise:

Try finding intervals on the piano with the minimum of hesitation - play any note and then locate a specified interval:

For example:

1) What is the perfect fifth of F?
2) What is the major sixth of E?
3) What is the diminished fifth (or tristep) of Bb?
4) What is the major seventh of Ab?
5) Of which note is D the major third?
6) Of which note is Gb the minor seventh?

N.B. This can also be practiced away from the piano.

(Answers at the end of chapter.)

INVERTING INTERVALS

The intervals shown in **Figure 1-6** were all located *above* the base note C. Intervals can also be located *below* a specified note, though this can lead to some confusion.

Consider the following intervals:

Figure 1-7

Q: We know that the interval between the note C and the E above is a major third. If the E were to be transposed down by an octave, would it still remain the major third of C?

A: Yes, E is clearly the major third of C within the context of a C major scale. But looking at the keyboard, we also notice that the interval between the two notes is now more than a major third. What is the new interval between E and C?

A: It is a minor sixth.

How can this be explained?

In the scale (or key) of C, E is the major third: this will always be true no matter where it is played on the keyboard. Though the interval between the two notes depend on the **register** chosen for each note, as shown in **Figure 1-7**.

It follows that E is the major third of C (the third degree of the major scale), while C is also the minor sixth of E (the sixth degree of the natural minor scale).

Please note the following:

• An interval can be inverted by transposing one of the two notes.

• All intervals and their inversions are related, since they contain the same degree of dissonance. The terms **consonance** and **dissonance** refer to the degree by which two notes, when played together, sound either consonant ("pure" or "in agreement"), or dissonant ("impure" or "jarring"). Both terms will prove crucial when we begin building jazz chords.

• The following simple rules apply when inverting intervals:

i) **major** becomes **minor**
ii) **minor** becomes **major**
iii) **perfect** remains **perfect**
iv) **tristep** remains **tristep**
v) **octave** remains **octave**

Exercise:

Practice inverting intervals at random and naming them accordingly.

TRIADS

Triads are the building blocks of Western harmony and they are formed by stacking one third on top of another. There are four possible stacking combinations:

a) **major third** on **minor third**
b) **minor third** on **major third**
c) **minor third** on **minor third**
d) **major third** on **major third**

The word "triad" is derived from the Greek word "tri-", which means "three." Each stacking combination has a name in classical theory:

a) **major triad**
b) **minor triad**
c) **diminished triad**
d) **augmented triad**

Figure 1-8

Major sounds cheerful and bold.

Minor sounds melancholic and pensive.

Diminished sounds dramatic and agitated.

Augmented sounds floating and mystical.

Exercise:

i) There are twelve major, minor, diminished and augmented triads, making a total of forty-eight triads to learn. Listen carefully to each triad, appraising its particular sound or "aura."

ii) Select at random a key in the right-hand and find *each* type of triad in succession.

iii) Select at random a key in the right-hand and find *one* specified triad.

INVERTING TRIADS

Triads can be **inverted** in exactly the same way as intervals by transposing up or down one or more of its constituent intervals. Whichever note is at the base of the triad will dictate its inversion. A triad can be played in one of three positions:

a) **Root position** (with the **tonic** at the base)
b) **First inversion** (with the **third** at the base)
c) **Second inversion** (with the **fifth** at the base)

Figure 1-9

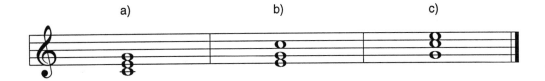

Exercises:

i) Selecting a major, minor, diminished or augmented triad at random, play the triad in root position, first and second inversion.

ii) Practice playing triads in both right and left hands.

CHORD SYMBOLS

A **chord** is the generic term used to described any combination of notes that are played simultaneously. Triads are therefore only one form of chord, though a very important one. They can be shown using the following symbols and abbreviations:

CHORD	SYMBOL	ABBREVIATION
C major triad	Cmaj	C
C minor triad	Cmin	Cm
C diminished triad	Cdim	C°
C augmented triad	Caug	C+

RANDOM PROGRESSIONS

Key literacy is an essential skill if we are to play good jazz piano. As well as understanding jazz theory, we must be able to implement this knowledge efficiently in all twelve keys, to be able to find all scales, intervals and triads in all keys with the minimum of hesitation.

In the following example, a chord progression is shown using a "random" combination triads. Try playing each triad at a steady pulse, gradually increase the tempo:

Example:

Cmaj / Dmin / Amin / A♭maj / Bbmin / Fmaj / Fdim / Gmin

Emaj / E♭aug / Bmin / D♭dim / Emin / Faug / F♯dim / etc.

Please note the following:

• Major and minor triads occur much more frequently than diminished and augmented triads, priority should therefore be given to learning major and minor triads.

• A useful tip is to **visualize** the shape of each triad on the keyboard, since there will be no time to calculate the constituent intervals of each triad when played under pressure.

Exercise:

Compose your own random chord progressions using a various combinations of major, minor, diminished and augmented triads.

THE TWELVE-BAR BLUES

The **twelve-bar blues** has provided the harmonic basis for much 20th century popular music, including rhythm and blues (R' n' B), boogie-woogie, rock-n-roll, as well as many bebop tunes composed in the 40s and 50s. These tunes were often based on the twelve-bar sequence, but introduced substitution chords for harmonic variety. We shall learn more about substitution chords later in the book, but in the meantime, the basic sequence can be played using major triads built on the tonic (I), fourth (IV) and fifth (V) of the major scale:

Figure 1-10

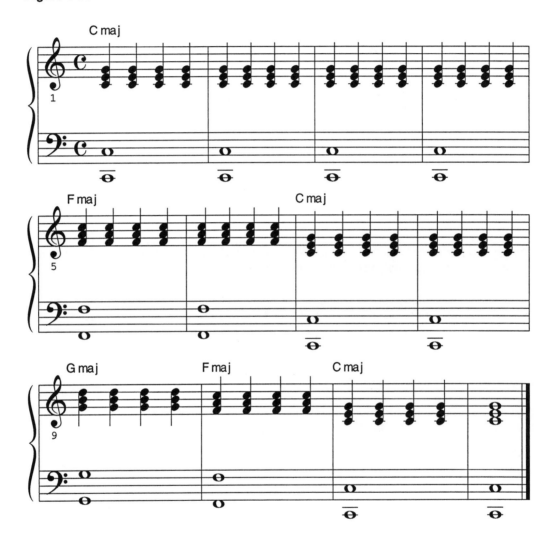

Exercise:

Transpose the above sequence into other keys using chords I, IV and V.

For example: a) G (I), C (IV) and D (V) in the key of G.
                    b) F (I), B♭ (IV) and C (V) in the key of F.
                    c) E♭ (I), A♭ (IV) and B♭ (V) in the key of E♭.

TRIADS AND INVERSIONS IN ALL KEYS

Figure 1-11

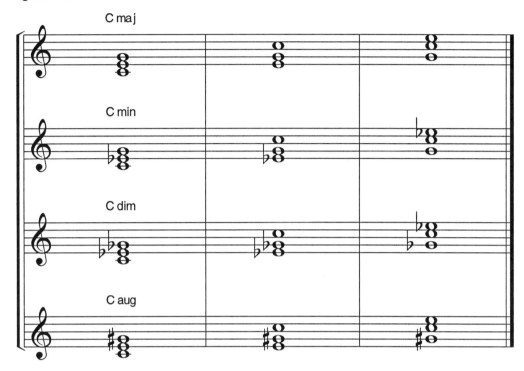

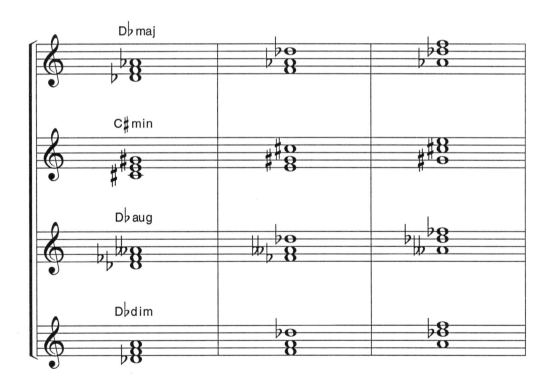

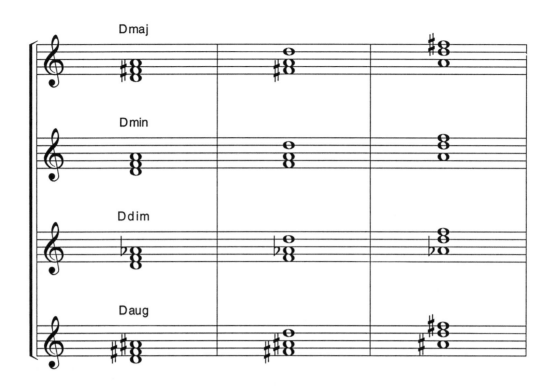

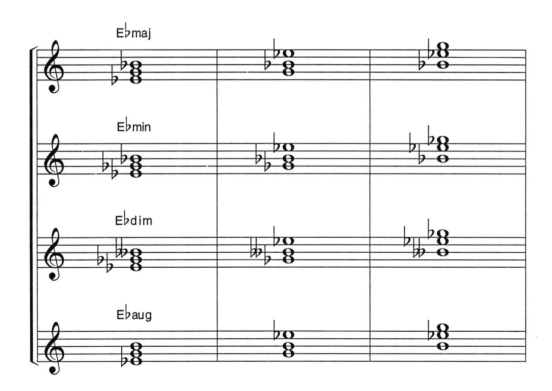

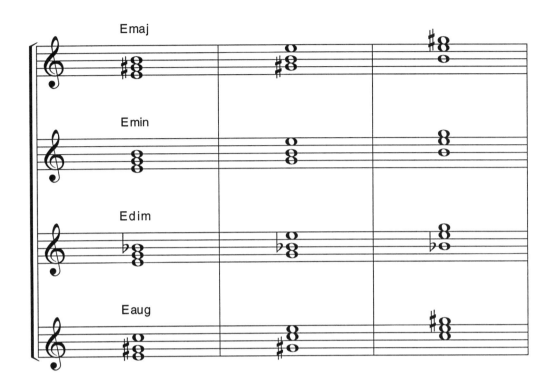

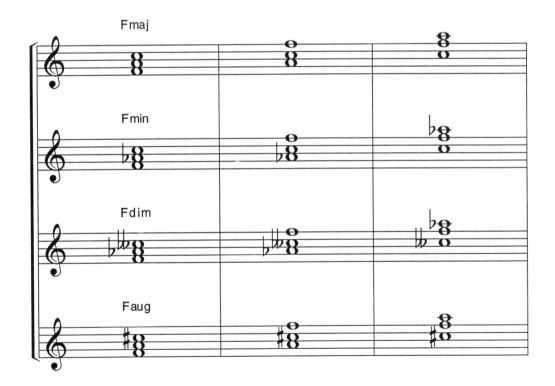

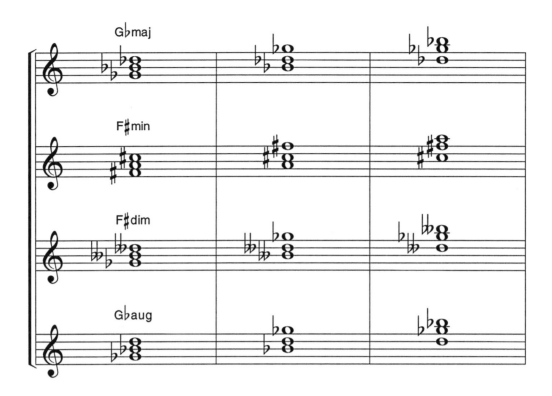

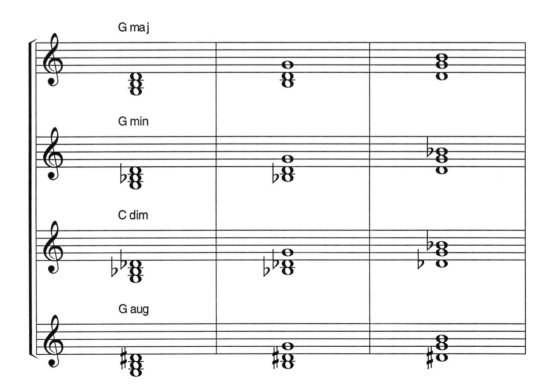

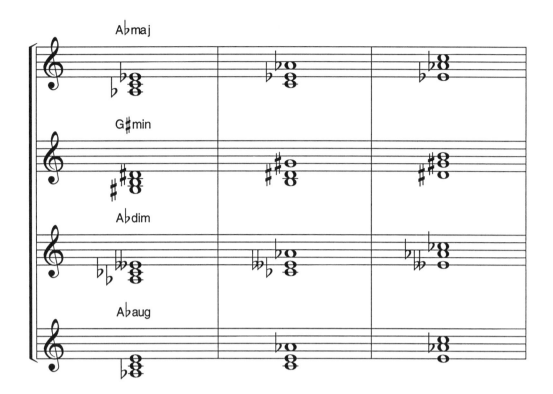

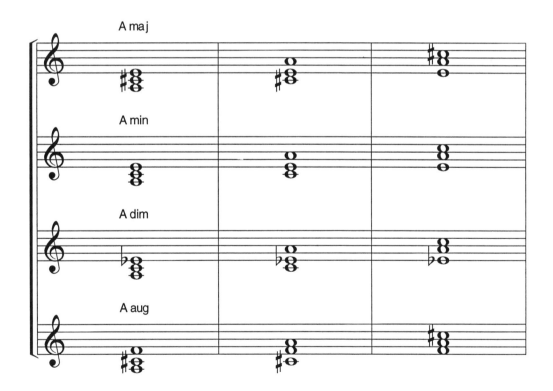

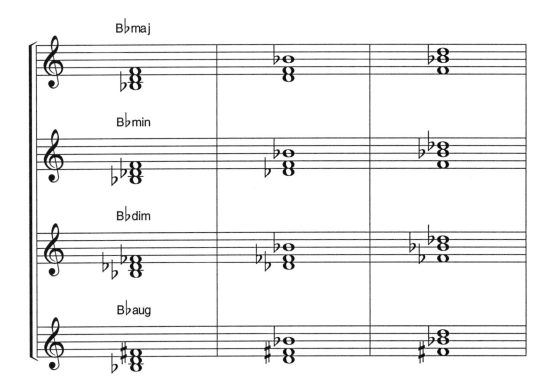

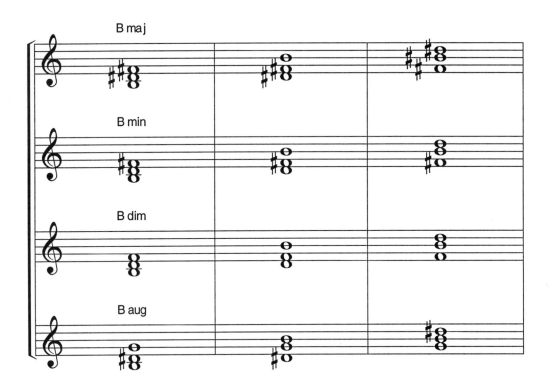

Answers to exercise on page 5 are as follows: C, C#, E, G, B♭, A♭.

CHAPTER TWO

JAZZ CHORDS

The triadic structure can now be extended by adding either a major sixth, minor seventh or major seventh to create **jazz chords**. By including one of these intervals a new harmonic palette is created, one that is more suggestive of jazz harmony. To make the learning process easier, we shall divide them into two groups: **primary** and **secondary** jazz chords.

FIVE PRIMARY JAZZ CHORDS

There are five **primary** jazz chords:

Figure 2-1

1) **Major seventh chord** (major triad + major 7th):

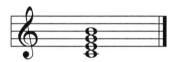

It is symbolized as either **Cmaj7**, **C△** or **CM7**, and consists of a major triad and a major seventh.

2) **Minor seventh chord** (minor triad + minor 7th):

It is symbolized as either **Cmin7**, **Cmi7**, **Cm7** or **C-7**, and consists of a minor triad and a minor seventh.

3) **Dominant seventh chord** (major triad + minor 7th):

It is symbolized as either **C7** or **Cdom7**, and consists of a major triad and a minor seventh.

4) **Half-diminished seventh chord** (diminished triad + minor 7th):

It is symbolized as either **Cø7** or **Cm7♭5**, and consists of a diminished triad and a minor seventh. It can also be referred to as a **minor seventh/flattened fifth chord**.

5) **Diminished seventh chord** (diminished triad + diminished seventh):

It is symbolized as either **Co7** or **Cdim7**, and consists of a diminished triad together with a diminished seventh (i.e. major sixth). It is a chord of crucial importance in diatonic harmony, since it is **symmetrical** dividing the octave into four equal parts, each of a minor third.

THE DOMINANT SEVENTH CHORD

The term **dominant** is a classical term used to describe the triad built on the fifth degree of the major scale (V). For example, G major is the dominant of C major. The dominant triad may include a minor seventh interval for a more emphatic sounding cadence, in which case will be referred to as a **dominant seventh** chord (cadences will be discussed in *Chapter Six*). However, the term "dominant seventh" can lead some to confusion when discussing jazz.

In jazz theory, the term is used to describe any seventh chord consisting of a major triad + a minor seventh interval, irrespective of its function or relationship to the tonic. To avoid any confusion, the dominant seventh chord is generally symbolized as a **seventh** chord:

Figure 2-2

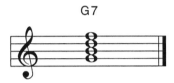

Exercises:

i) Beginning on C, play each primary chord ascending the chromatic scale:

Figure 2-3

ii) Select at random any note and find all five primary jazz chords.

iii) Select at random any note and find one specified primary jazz chord.

iv) Compose a random chord progression beginning on any note, comprising a random combination of primary jazz chords, as suggested by the following example:

CΔ I Am7 I B♭7 I Em7 I D∅7 I A♭m7 I B°7 I G♭7 I CΔ etc.

v) Play the your random chord progression with the left-hand.

vi) Play your random chord progression repeating the chord in the right-hand on each beat of the bar, accompanied by the tonic of each chord (as an octave) in the left-hand, as shown in the following example:

Figure 2-4

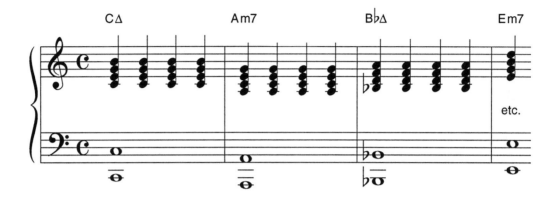

INVERTING PRIMARY JAZZ CHORDS

In *Chapter One* we learned how triads could be played in one of three positions: in **root position**, first inversion and **second inversion**. Inversions are particularly useful when a series of triads is played in succession, since they can be used to produce a smoother harmonic line by restricting unnecessary movement in the right-hand:

Figure 2-5

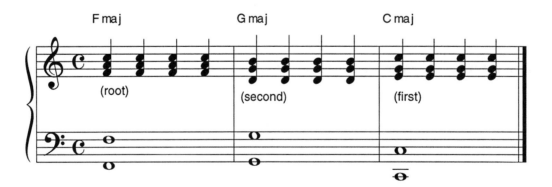

Similarly, jazz chords can be inverted, but there will now be a **third** inversion created by the additional fourth interval.

For example, C7 can be played either in root position or one of three inversions:

Figure 2-6

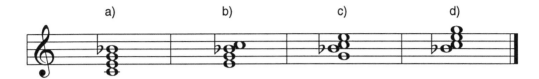

a) in **root** position
b) in **first** inversion
c) in **second** inversion
d) in **third** inversion

In the following example, a smoother harmonic line is created by introducing inversions that minimise the movement when moving between chords. This refers to the classical principle of good **voice-leading**:

Figure 2-7

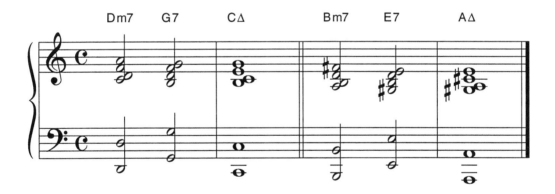

Principles of good voice leading:

• The same notes in consecutive chords should be played in the same register. These are referred to as **common tones** in classical theory.

• Changing notes in consecutive chords should proceed to the nearest available note.

• When playing progressions, think "horizontally" as well as "vertically." Imagine each tone as representing a voice with its own melodic line, and a chord as being a vertical layer of voices.

FIVE SECONDARY JAZZ CHORDS

The five primary chords shown previously are the most frequently used in jazz, but there are other chords that can be derived from the triadic structure + an auxiliary interval - we shall refer to this group as **secondary** jazz chords. They are formed in exactly the same way as primary jazz chords, but include *augmented* and *diminished* triads. Collectively, there are ten jazz chords that can be derived from the triadic structure + an auxiliary interval.

There are five **secondary** jazz chords:

Figure 2-8

6) **Augmented major seventh** (augmented triad + major 7th):

It is symbolized as **Caug△** or **C+△**, and consists of an augmented triad and a major seventh. It is most often found in contemporary jazz scores.

7) **Augmented seventh** (augmented triad + minor 7th):

It is symbolized as **Caug7** or **C+7**, and consists of an augmented triad and a minor seventh. The "+" sign refers to the fifth and *not* to the seventh of the chord.

8) **Minor-major seventh** (minor triad + major 7th):

It is symbolized as **Cm△**, **C-△** or **Cm#7**, and consists of a minor triad and a major seventh. It sounds fairly dissonant in its present form, but will have an important harmonic application at a later stage.

9) **Major sixth** (major triad + major 6th):

It is symbolized as **C6** or **Cmaj6**, and consists of a major triad and a major sixth. It is often written at the beginning or the end of a song where the melody note is the tonic, thereby averting the dissonance that would otherwise occur by playing the tonic and the major seventh simultaneously.

10) **Minor sixth** (minor triad + major sixth):

It is symbolized as **Cm6**, **C-6**, **Cmi6** or **Cmin6**, and consists of a minor triad and a major sixth. It is often found in the chord charts of songs written in a minor key.

THE SUSPENDED FOURTH CHORD

A chord that is not included in the ten primary and secondary jazz chords, but is often found in chord charts is the **suspended fourth** chord:

Figure 2-9

It is generally symbolized as **C7sus** or **C7sus 4**. The term "sus" is an abbreviation for "suspension" or "suspended" and refers to the classical device of suspending, or holding over, a note from the one chord to another within a cadence. However, in jazz a *suspension* can be created by replacing the third in a seventh chord with a fourth. Invariably, this suspended chord is followed by a regular seventh chord, referred to as its *resolution*.

Exercises:

i) Select at random any note and find all ten primary and secondary jazz chords.

ii) Select at random any note and find one specified primary or secondary jazz chord.

iii) Select at random any note and find one specific primary or secondary jazz chord
playing it first in root position, and then in first, second and third inversion.

Task:

Outlined below is the chord progression of Richard Rodgers and Oscar Hammerstein II's
"Getting to Know You". Try playing the chord progression using the jazz chords shown so far
in this chapter:

‖   C6   F7 | Em7   Am7 | Dm7   G7 | Dm7   G7 |

‖   Dm7   G7 | Dm7   G7 | CΔ | Dm7   G7   ‖

‖   C6   F7 | Em7   Am7 | FΔ | F6 |

| Am7 | D7 | Dm7 | G7   ‖

‖   C6   F7 | Em7   Am7 | Dm7   G7 | Dm7   G7 |

‖   Dm7   G7 | Dm7   G7 | C7 | Gm7   C7   ‖

‖   FΔ | Dm7   G7 | E7 | Am7 |

| Dm7 | G7 | C6 | Am7   D7 |

| Dm7 | G7 | C6 | ′/.   ‖

Having become familiar with the chord progression itself, the melody can now be introduced in the right-hand accompanied by chords in the left-hand. Inversions can also be played in the left-hand to minimise unnecessary movement and to provide a smoother harmonic line:

Figure 2-10

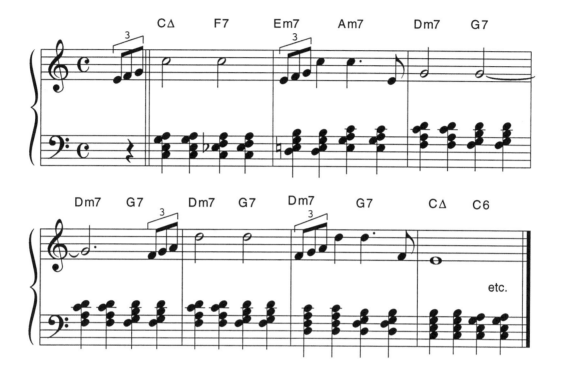

PROCEDURE

Choose a song that does not contain too many chords and adopt the following procedure:

a) Play the melody together with single bass notes in the left-hand as suggested by the chord symbols.

b) Play the chord progression as shown in **Figure 2-7**.

c) Play the melody accompanied by chords in the left-hand as shown in **Figure 2-10**.

Please note the following:

• When playing chord progressions, **extension intervals** should be ignored for the time being. For example: the chord symbol C7#9 should be simply interpreted as C7.

• The chord symbol C (i.e. C major triad) can usually be interpreted either as CΔ or C6, while the chord symbol Cm (i.e. C minor triad) can usually be interpreted as either Cm7 or Cm6.

• This is a good moment to become better acquainted with the classic songs of Jerome Kern, Cole Porter, George Gershwin, Richard Rodgers, Irving Berlin, Harold Arlen and many others. Referred to collectively as **standards**, these songs are gems of musical construction and are ideal for harmonisation using primary and secondary jazz chords.

• This would also be a good moment to purchase a songbook displaying only the melodic line and accompanying chord symbols (without piano accompaniments). They are sometimes referred to as "Real Books" and there are several good publications currently available.

RECOMMENDED SONGBOOKS

• **The Real Jazz Book**, published by Hal Leonard Publishing Corp.

• **The Best Chord Changes For The Most Requested Standards**, by Frank Mantooth, published by Hal Leonard Publishing Corp.

• **The Best Chord Changes For The World's Greatest Standards**, by Frank Mantooth, published by Hal Leonard Publishing Corp.

• **The Best Chord Changes For The Best Ever Standards**, by Frank Mantooth, published by Hal Leonard Publishing Corp.

• **The Best Chord Changes For The Best Known Songs**, by Frank Mantooth, published by Hal Leonard Publishing Corp.

CHAPTER THREE

THREE-PART HARMONY

The jazz chords in the previous chapter were shown in **closed position**, that is to say, the constituent intervals were played as close together as possible, i.e. within the same octave. Approaching the chords in this way gives a clear insight into the rudiments of jazz harmony, though a jazz pianist would rarely play them in such a simplistic way, rather they would rearrange the constituent intervals to take advantage of the rich and varied sonorities offered by the piano. In this chapter, we shall see how jazz chords can be played in **open position**.

PLAYING CHORDS IN OPEN-POSITION

The term **voicing** is the generic term used to describe the precise placement of the notes within a chord. In the first instance, we can transpose the tonic down an octave to create a more sonorous sounding chord:

Figure 3-1

The chord is now in **open-position**, since the constituent intervals are no longer played as closely together as possible.

OMITTING THE FIFTH

Though this chord sounds musically satisfactory when played in isolation, it will quickly become apparent that it is less than satisfactory when played as part of a chord progression. To play chord progressions in open-position, we shall begin by playing the minimum notes needed to "define" the chord.

Consider the following:

Primary and second jazz chords all contain the following constituent intervals:

• tonic
• third (minor or major)
• fifth (perfect, diminished or augmented)
• sixth or seventh (minor or major)

The most frequently used chords in jazz are the major seventh, minor seventh and seventh chord - they are distinguishable from eachother by alterations to the third and seventh, while the fifth remains constant (perfect) for all three chords. Should the fifth be omitted from the chords, they will still be clearly identifiable.

In the following example, the fifth has been omitted from the C7 chord, creating two alternative voicings:

Figure 3-2

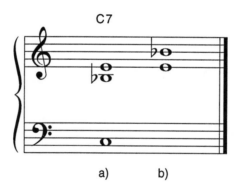

Please note the following:

• We shall refer to these alternative voicings as a) and b):

Voicing a) consists of the *tonic, seventh* and *third* (played as a tenth).

Voicing b) consists of the *tonic, third* and *seventh* (played as an octave + a seventh).

• The chord is clearly heard as C7 despite the absence of the fifth. The same would be true for the CΔ and Cm7 chords.

• The fifth is the second harmonic in the **harmonic series** and is already present in the tonic (bass note). For this reason the absence of the fifth is barely audible.

• The C∅7 and C°7 chords can also be played in three parts (without the fifth), though their harmonic definition will be ambiguous.

PROCEDURE FOR FINDING THREE-PART CHORDS

Three-part chords are the building blocks of jazz harmony and must be thoroughly learned in all keys. To make this process easier, we shall begin by learning only the major seventh, minor seventh and seventh chords adopting the following procedure:

Procedure:

a) Select the **tonic** in the left-hand, then find the octave above with the right-hand.
b) Descend in the right-hand to either the **minor** or **major seventh** interval (half-step or step).
c) Then find the **minor** or **major third** of the tonic above the octave and play voicing a).
d) Then transpose the seventh in the right-hand up an octave and play voicing b).

A good practice routine is to play each chord **ascending** the chromatic scale:

Figure 3-3

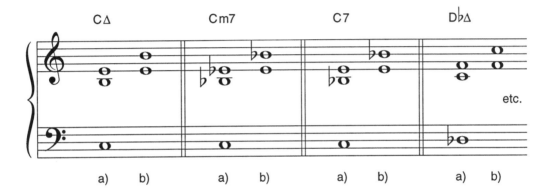

Exercises:

i) Play the above progression, ascending and descending the chromatic scale.

ii) Select at random any note of the scale and play *each* of the chords shown above.

iii) Select at random any note of the scale and play *one* specific chord.

Please note the following:

• This is a good moment to begin thinking of chords "visually" as well as "aurally," memorizing their individual shapes on the keyboard.

• Compare the sonority of the open-position three-part chords shown above with the closed-position chords from the previous chapter? They clearly have a lighter and more open sound - one that is better suited for jazz piano?

• Three-part chords in all twelve keys are shown at the end of this chapter.

VOICE-LEADING IN THREE PARTS

Having learned to play major seventh, minor seventh and seventh chords in all twelve keys using the voicings shown in **Figure 3-3**, the three-part harmonic process should be brought to a logical conclusion:

*When moving between three-part chords, the **nearest** voicing of each subsequent chord should be sought to create a smooth harmonic line.*

In the following example, the Dm7 chord is played in voicing a), moving to the **nearest** voicing of G7 which is voicing b), ending on the nearest voicing of C△ which is voicing a):

Figure 3-4

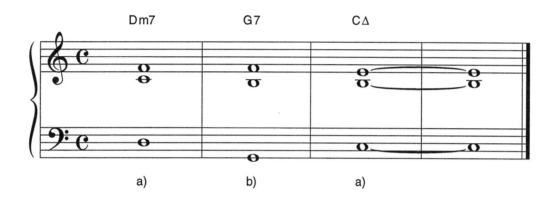

The above progression could also have begun on voicing b) of the Dm7 chord, then moved to voicing a) of G7, ending on voicing b) of C△:

Figure 3-5

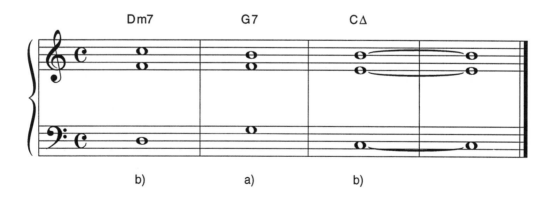

Summary:

The fifth has been omitted for the following reasons:

• The process of moving from one chord to the nearest inversion of the next refers to the classical principle of **voice-leading**.   The aim is to create a "seamless flow of harmony", where the chords flow from one to another without a perceptible break in the harmonic line. Omitting the fifth makes for a smoother transition between chords.

• The fifth creates a degree of "inertia" to the harmonic flow when playing chord progressions, due to its harmonic function of reinforcing the tonic. By omitting it, each chord has a softer and less strident sound, one that is better suited to playing jazz chord progressions.

• It is interesting to note that the building blocks of classical harmony are triads (tonic, third, fifth), while in jazz harmony they are also a three-part structure (tonic, third, seventh).

• The fifth will be reintroduced at a later stage, not as an essential part of each chord, but as one of several intervals that may be chosen when building four and five-part chords.

Exercises:

i) Beginning with any major seventh, minor seventh or seventh chord, find the nearest three-part voicing of another chord chosen at random.

ii) Shown here is a chord progression using distinctly jazz-orientated patterns. Play it using the 4/4 pulse shown in **Figure 3-6**.

Example 3-1:

```
‖  F∆  | Em7  A7 |   Dm7  |   D♭7  | Cm7  F7 |  B♭∆  |

| B♭m7  E♭7 |   A♭∆  | Am7  D7 | Bm7  E7 |  E♭∆  |   D∆  |

| C#m7  F#7 |   B∆  ‖
```

Figure 3-6

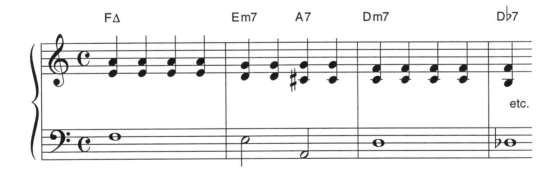

THE VOICING SHIFT

If the voicing-leading principle of moving to the nearest voicing of each subsequent chord is observed too strictly, the chords will frequently move to a lower and lower register of the piano, particularly if the progression is based on the **cycle of fifths**.

The cycle of fifths and cadences will be discussed in *Chapter Six*. For the time being, it will suffice to say that many standard chord progressions are based on the cycle of fifths, whereby each chord proceeds to a subsequent chord "built on its fifth degree."

For Example:

| D | G | C | F | B♭ | etc.

N.B. D is the fifth of G, G is the fifth of C, C is the fifth of F, F is the fifth of Bb...

The chord progression of a standard song typically consists of fragments of the cycle of fifths being constantly **interrupted** and **transposed**. Playing the nearest voicing each time will result in voicings moving down the keyboard, it will therefore be necessary to interrupt this process and select a voicing higher up the keyboard. This we shall refer to as a **voicing shift**.

The trick is to introduce the voicing shift *where it is least perceptible*, between II-V and II-V-I cadences or melodic phrases. Shifting the voicing enables all the chords to be played in the same register of the keyboard, where the chords sound most sonorous and supportive to the melody. Ideally, the right-hand seventh and third should be around or just below middle C.

In the following example, the harmonic line is interrupted by a voicing shift between bars 4 and 5, before the final II-V-I cadence. The result is that all the chords in the progression are played within the same register of the keyboard:

Figure 3-7

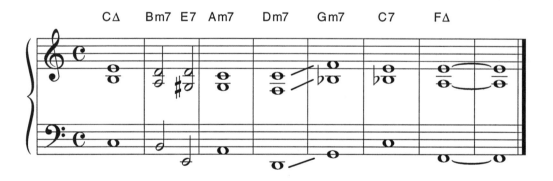

*N.B. The same distance is maintained between the two hands throughout the example - either a **seventh** or a **tenth** (octave + third).*

THREE-PART PRIMARY AND SECONDARY JAZZ CHORDS

To interpret the chord progression of a standard song, it will be necessary to find a way of playing both primary and secondary jazz chords in three parts. This can simply be done by omitting the fifth from all the chords, including those with diminished or augmented fifths:

Three-part voicings for all primary and secondary jazz chords are as follows:

Figure 3-8

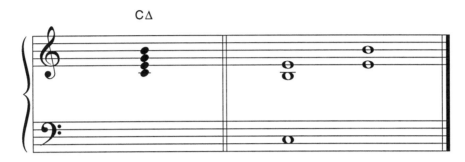

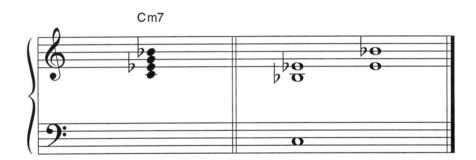

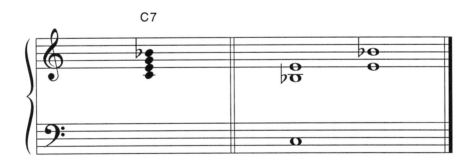

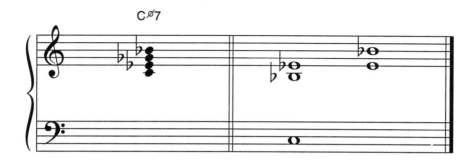

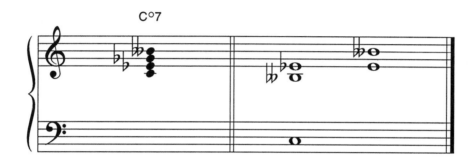

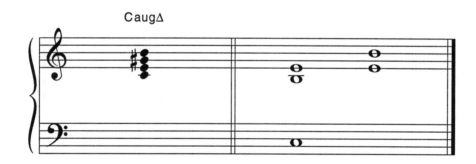

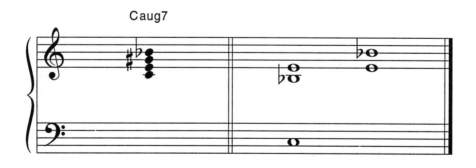

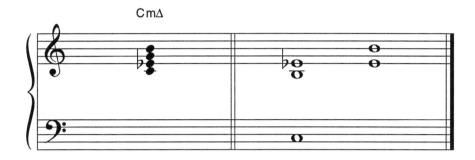

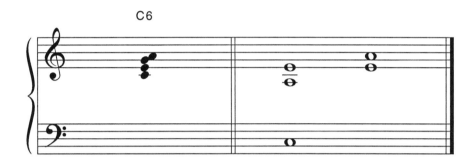

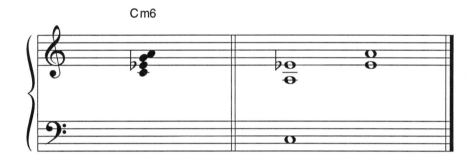

The suspended fourth chord (sus4 or sus) can also be played in three-parts:

Figure 3-9

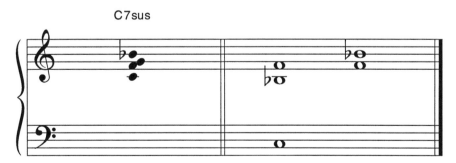

Please note the following:

• Some of the secondary jazz chords are clearly indistinguishable from primary jazz chords when played in three parts. For example: CaugΔ is the same as CΔ, Caug7 is the same as C7. When playing chord progressions that include secondary jazz chords, a degree of harmonic ambiguity is quite acceptable.

• Resist the temptation to insert an occasional fourth part at this stage, since it will interrupt the flow of the harmony in three-parts.

In the following example, a chordal accompaniment for Victor Young and Ned Washington's "Stella By Starlight" is shown using only three-part chords. Notice that voicings chosen lie just below the melodic line and that voicing shifts occur at several places to maintain the chords within the same area of the keyboard:

Figure 3-10

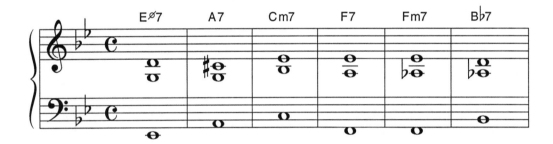

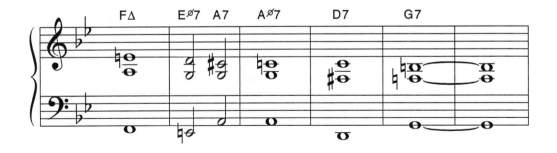

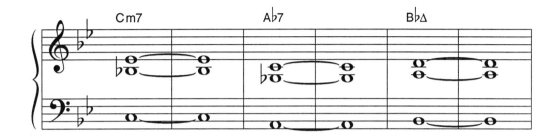

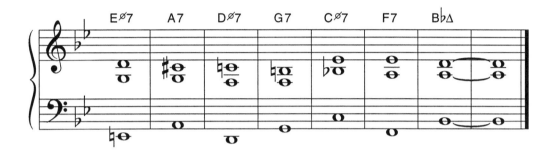

Exercises:

i) Compose a random chord progression similar to **Example 3-1**, consisting of a combination of primary and secondary jazz chords. Beginning on either voicing a) or b), proceed to the nearest voicing of each subsequent chord. Remember that it may be necessary to introduce a voicing shift from time to time, should the chords get too low down or too high up the keyboard.

ii) Select a song similar to the one shown above and play the chord progression using three-part chords. Try to maintain the chords just *below* the melodic line within the most sonorous area of the keyboard.

CHORD CHART FOR MAJOR SEVENTH, MINOR SEVENTH AND DOMINANT SEVENTH CHORDS IN THREE PARTS

Figure 3-11

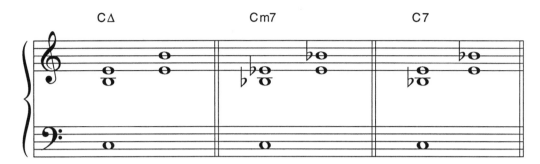

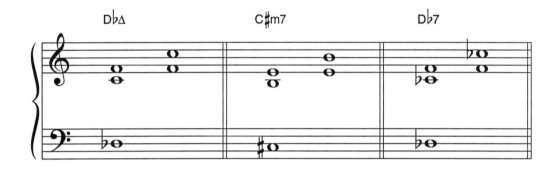

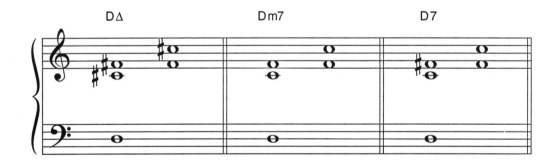

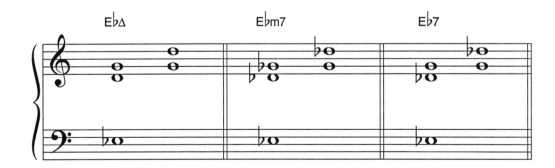

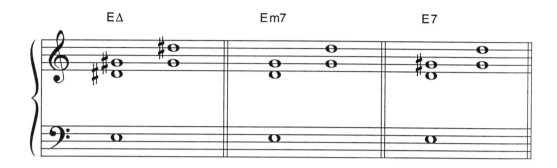

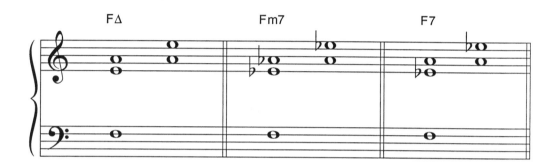

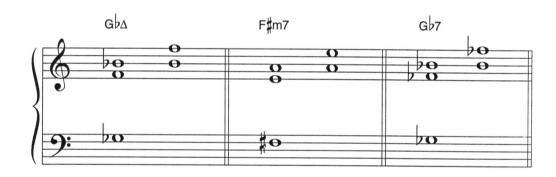

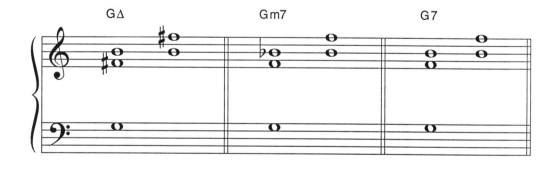

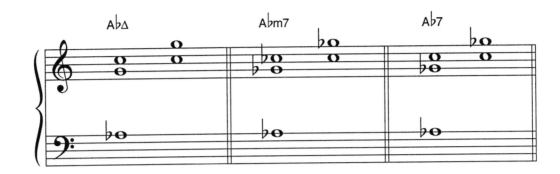

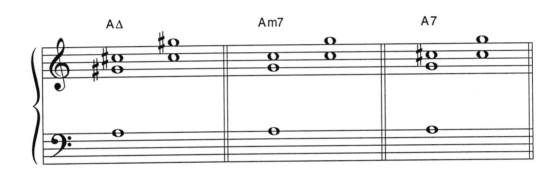

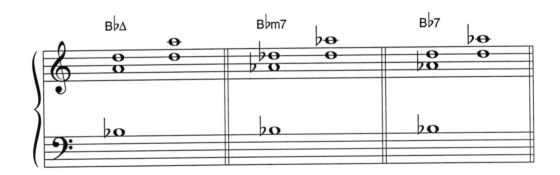

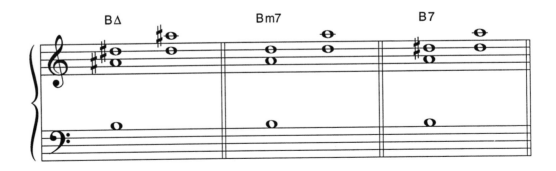

CHAPTER FOUR

ACCOMPANIMENT MODELS

In this chapter, we shall introduce a series of **accompaniment models** to help us become more efficient at playing three-part chord progressions in all keys, while providing an insight into various jazz styles. The models are ideal for accompanying songs where only the melodic line and chord symbols are shown.

INTERPRETING CHORD PROGRESSIONS IN THREE PARTS

Looking through any songbook will reveal chord symbols that need further clarification, we must therefore learn how to "simplify" each chord progression to bring it within our immediate grasp and knowledge. Shown here are a selection of symbols and performance directions that might be found in a standard chord chart, together with an explanation of how they might best be interpreted when playing in three parts.

1) Chord symbols often include **auxiliary** or **extension** intervals (♭5, ♭9 , ♯9 and ♯11) that are customarily placed slightly raised after the chord . However, playing these intervals is **not obligatory** and should be omitted for the time being.

In the following example, C7♭9 is simply interpreted as C7 in three-parts:

Figure 4-1

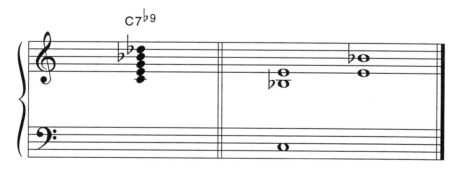

2) When two chords appear in the same bar, they should be played on beats one and three:

Figure 4-2

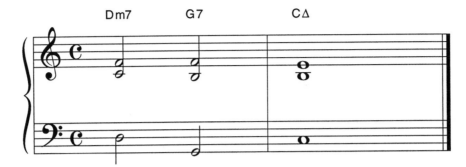

3) Simple rhythmic displacements can be indicated by **slashes** above or below the chord symbol. In the following example, the Dm7 chord has three slashes beneath it, while the G7 chord has one, indicating that three beats should be allocated to the first chord and one beat to the second:

Figure 4-3

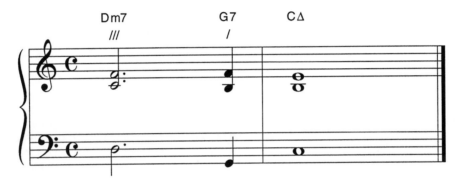

4) More complex rhythmic displacements can best be shown using musical notation. In the following example, the G7 chord anticipates the third beat by an eighth note:

Figure 4-4

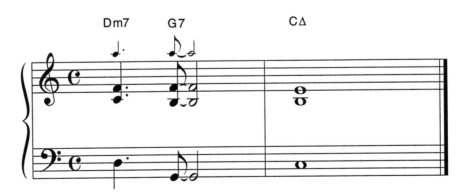

5) When playing a chordal accompaniment, the register chosen for the right-hand voicing should generally lie just below middle C.

In the following example, the voicings chosen lie just below the melodic line, harmonically "supporting" rather than "interfering" with the melody. Accompaniment voicings sound best when played in this lower-to-middle register of the piano, though they may sound a little muddy when played without the melody:

Figure 4-5

PLAYING JAZZ STANDARDS

To play an accompaniment on the piano will require a rudimentary knowledge of jazz harmony and an understanding of the various song forms that make up the standard repertoire.

"Standards" generally fall into four broad categories:

1) **Ballad**	-	Slow tempo, often characterized by more than one chord per bar, many great songs were originally conceived as ballads.
		Examples: "My Funny Valentine" "Round Midnight" "Body and Soul"

2) **Swing**   -   Slow/medium tempo, often characterized by
                                                     more than one chord per bar, the melody
                                                     may appear to be less dense than a ballad.

                                                     Examples: "Just In Time"
                                                                   "Out Of Nowhere"
                                                                   "In A Mellow Tone"

                               -                    Fast tempo, often characterized by one chord
                                                     bar (or two bars), the melody may appear even
                                                     less dense (the exception being the highly
                                                     complex bebop tunes, most famously written
                                                     by Charlie Parker).

                                                     Examples: "Cherokee" (may also be played medium)
                                                                   "Love for Sale" ("   )
                                                                   "Ornithology" (Charlie Parker)

3) **Waltz**   -   Waltzes can be played at almost any tempo but
                                                     are usually played medium, often characterized
                                                     by one chord per bar.

                                                     Examples: "Someday My Prince Will Come"
                                                                   "Alice in Wonderland"
                                                                   "Bluesette"

4) **Latin**   -   **Bossa nova**, **samba** and **salsa** are the forms
                                                     of Latin music most often played by jazz pianists.
                                                     Bossa nova is the ballad form of samba, which is
                                                     a dance. Latin music can be played at any tempo
                                                     and is characterized by one or two chords per bar.
                                                     Many of the best bossa nova themes were written
                                                     in the 50's and 60's by Antonio Carlos Jobim.

                                                     Examples: "Girl from Ipenema"
                                                                   "Desafinado"
                                                                   "One Note Samba"

Please note the following:

• In some songbooks, the style of song is clearly indicated (ballad, medium swing, latin etc.).
The approximate tempo may also be shown (quarter note = 120).

• If nothing is indicated, the style will have to be deduced from the time signature, melodic and
harmonic style, composer, and with reference to any recordings that can be obtained.

• Remember that these are very broad categories and that a song can be interpreted in
almost any style. For example: a song originally conceived as a slow tempo swing could also
be played as a bossa nova, or a ballad could be played as a medium tempo swing etc.

BINARY AND TERNARY RHYTHM

Jazz is mostly played in **ternary** rhythm (triplets) as opposed to **binary** rhythm (duplets), it is this factor that gives jazz its characteristic "swing" feel. A more technical explanation is that the eighth notes in a melodic phrase should be played as if they were triplets with the first two notes of each group of three being tied together. This creates a "lilt" to the eighth-note rhythm that is between **even** and **dotted**.

Figure 4-6

Binary:

Ternary:

or,

Please note the following:

• An alternative way of writing jazz would be in 12/8 time, but this would make it unnecessarily complicated. Jazz is therefore written in binary rhythm with the understanding that the melody should be played in ternary rhythm, as if it were written in 12/8 time.

• Jazz is usually played in **ternary** rhythm (swing eighth notes), whereas fusion, funk and latin music is usually played in **binary** rhythm (straight eighth notes).

ACCOMPANIMENT MODELS

Outlined below are a series of accompaniment models for playing **ballads**, **fast** and **slow swing** tempos, **waltzes**, **bossa nova** and **cabaret** styles. They are based on a II-V-I cadence in C major and can be played for chord progressions in three parts.

• TRADITIONAL

The first model is based on a traditional **stomp** as played in early *Dixieland* jazz. The strong pronouncement of each-beat-of-the-bar is suggestive of a march and is typical of early jazz, as might have been heard in New Orleans in the 20's and 30's:

Figure 4-7

• The model can be elaborated by alternating the bass notes between the tonic and its dominant (fifth) on the third beat of each bar. This is also suggestive of an early jazz style:

Figure 4-8

Bass notes can be both **repeated** and **syncopated** when played against the constant chordal rhythm. In the following example, the bass note is repeated on the half-beat prior to the dominant on the last beat of each bar. This radically alters the rhythm feel of the model:

Figure 4-9

A simple **walking** bass line can be played with a combination of scales and chord tones based on each chord, as the following example demonstrates:

Figure 4-10

Exercises:

i) Choose a standard song and play an accompaniment in three-parts referring to each of the accompaniment models shown above.

ii) Try and find another musicians to play the melody for you, alternatively try singing or humming the melody above the chords.

iii) Use a **metronome** to develop your rhythmic awareness. Begin slowly and gradually increase the tempo.

• STRIDE PIANO

The **stride piano** style evolved from **ragtime**. It is characterized by alternating between the bass note and the chord, the bass notes also alternate between the tonic and fifth. A master stride pianist would typically play both the bass and the chords in the left-hand, thereby leaving the right-hand free to play the melody:

Figure 4-11

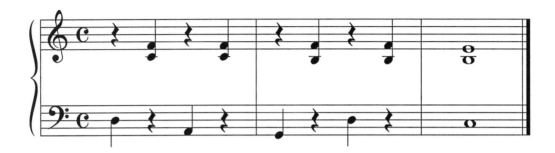

• WALTZ

A **waltz** is always played in 3/4 time (three beats in a bar). It is characterized by the bass note being played on the first beat of the bar, with the chord being played on the second and third beats:

Figure 4-12

The **Viennese waltz** is characterized by slightly anticipating (bringing forward) the chord that falls on the second beat of the bar. The degree by which this chord is anticipated will characterize the waltz:

Figure 4-13

The **jazz waltz** is similar to the Viennese waltz, but with an additional bass note played half way through each bar, thereby creating a syncopated two-against-three effect between the bass notes and the chords:

Figure 4-14

A walking bass line can also be introduced, though the character of the waltz will be less discernible due to the loss of syncopation between the bass notes and the chords:

Figure 4-15

• SWING

The **swing era** was when swing and dance bands were at the vanguard of popular music. These included the legendary bands of Duke Ellington, Count Basie, Glenn Miller, Benny Goodman and Tommy Dorsey etc. Nowadays, the term **swing** is used generically to describe most jazz played in a swing style. One characteristic of the big band sound is the "stabbing" of chords by the horn sections (trumpets, saxophones and trombones) when accompanying a soloist. Though it is difficult to recreate this on the piano, an approximation can be made.

In the following example, **stabbing chords** are played with syncopation suggestive of a horn section accompanying a soloist:

Figure 4-16

Combining the walking bass line from **Figure 4-10** with the chords from **Figure 4-16** will result in a convincing swing accompaniment, suggestive of a double-bass and a chordal instrument (piano or guitar) playing at a medium swing tempo:

Figure 4-17

• BOSSA NOVA

Bossa nova was created in Brazil, the two most prominent exponents being the composer Antonio Carlos Jobim and singer/guitarist João Gilberto. This music became enormously popular in English-speaking countries in the 60's through collaborations with the saxophonist Stan Getz, and the singers Astrid Gilberto and Frank Sinatra. It is essentially guitar-based, though it can be approximated on the piano.

In the following example, syncopated chords are accompanied by bass notes played on beats one and three. The syncopation effect created by anticipating the first beat of each bar (or alternate bar) is quintessential to the bossa nova rhythm. When playing latin music it is essential to observe where the rhythmic stresses fall - which chords are played *long* and which are played *short*.

Figure 4-18

An alternative bossa nova rhythm that includes a syncopated bass line can be created by anticipating the fifth (dominant) in alternate bars:

Figure 4-19

There are numerous variations to the rhythms shown here. To really assimilate the style it is essential to listen to the original recordings made by Tom Jobim and João Gilberto in the 50's and 60's. The value of making an in-depth study of this music cannot be overstated for jazz pianists - though it is guitar based, its language can teach us an enormous amount about jazz harmony, in particular about the importance of voice-leading when accompanying a vocal line.

• CABARET

Finally, an accompaniment model that is evocative of the way show tunes were accompanied in the 30's and 40's can be created by doubling the outer notes of the right-hand voicing (third or seventh) and sustaining them throughout the bar, while simultaneously alternating between the bass notes and the remaining part of the chord (third or seventh). The bass notes should also alternate between the tonic and fifth. This is a particularly useful style for accompanying singers in show tunes or when playing in a theatrical or music hall style, it can also be played extremely fast!

Figure 4-20

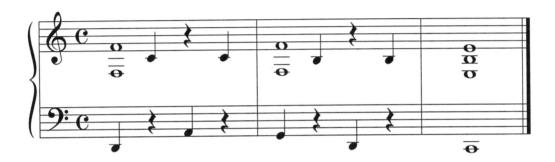

or alternatively:

Figure 4-21

Please note the following:

• The accompaniment models shown in this chapter are all three bars long - the first two bars can be repeated over and over again until the rhythms becomes fluent.

• They should then be transposed into all twelve keys.

• Try also singing or humming the melodies while playing the accompanying chords.

SONGS TO SELECT

Most of the following songs can all be found in **The Real Jazz Book**, published by Hal Leonard Publishing Corp. and available from all good music shops:

A Child Is Born (Thad Jones)
Alice In Wonderland (Sammy Fain and Bob Hilliard)
All the Things You Are (Jerome Kern and Oscar Hammerstein)
Autumn in New York (Veronon Duke)
Autumn Leaves (Joseph Korma and Johnny Mercer)
Blame It On My Youth (Oscar Levant and Edward Heyman)
Darn That Dream (Jimmy van Heusen and Eddie DeLange)
Days of Wine and Roses (Henry Mancini and Johnny Mercer)
Detour Ahead (Herb Ellis, John Frigo and Lou Carter)
Dolphin Dance (Herbie Hancock)
Dream Dancing (Cole Porter)
Early Autumn (Ralph Burns, Woody Herman, and Johnny Mercer)
Easy Living (Leo Robin and Ralph Rainger)
Everything Happens To Me (Matt Dennis and Tom Adair)
Georgia on My Mind (Hoagy Carmichael and Stuart Gorrell)
Girl Talk (Neal Hefti and Bobby Troup)
Gone With The Wind (Allie Wrubel and Herb Magidson)
Guess I'll Hang My Tears Out To Dry (Jule Styne and Sammy Cahn
I Remember You (Victor Schertzinger and Johnny Mercer)
I Thought About You (Jimmy Van Heusen and Johnny Mercer)
I'm Old Fashioned (Jerome Kern and Johnny Mercer)
If I Should Lose You (Leo Robin and Ralph Rainger)
If You Never Come Back To Me (Antonio Carlos Jobim and Ray Gilbert)
Imagination (Jimmy van Heusen and Johnny Burke)
In a Sentimental Mood (Duke Ellington, Irving Mills and Manny Kurtz)
Invitation (Bronislau Kaper and Paul Francis Webster)
It Could Happen to You (Jimmy Van Heusen and Johnny Burke)
Like someone in Love (Jimmy Van Heusen and Johnny Burke)
Lover (Richard Rodgers and Lorenz Hart)
Lullaby of Birdland (George Shearing and George David Weiss)
Makin' Whoopee (Walter Donaldson and Gus Kahn)
My Foolish Heart (Victor Young and Ned Washington)
My Ideal (Richard A. Whiting, Newell Chase and Leo Robin)
My Old Flame (Sam Coslow and Arthur Johnston)
My Romance (Richard Rodgers and Lorenz Hart)
Never Let Me Go (Ray Evans and Jay Livingston)
On Green Dolphin Street (Bronislau Kaper and Ned Washington)
Once I Loved (Antonio Carlos Jobim and Ray Gilbert)
Out Of Nowhere (Johnny Green and Edward Heyman)
Prelude to a Kiss (Duke Ellington, Irving Gordon and Irving Mills)
Someday My Prince Will Come (Frank Churchill)
Sophisticated Lady (Duke Ellington, Irving Mills and Mitchell Parish)
Stella by Starlight (Victor Young and Ned Washington)
Tangerine (Victor Schertzinger and Johnny Mercer)
Teach Me Tonight (Gene DePaul and Sammy Cahn)
The Blue Room (Richard Rodgers and Lorenz Hart)
The Folks Who Live on the Hill (Jerome Kern and Oscar Hammerstein II)
The Nearness of You (Hoagy Carmichael and Ned Washington)
The Shadow of Your Smile (Johnny Mandel and Francis Webster)
Too Late Now (Burton Lane and Alan Jay Lerner)
Wave (Antonio Carlos Jobim)
We'll Be Together Again (Carl Fischer and Frankie Laine)
Without A Song (Vincent Newmans, Wiliam Rose and Edward Eliscu)
You Are Too Beautiful (Richard Rodgers and Lorenz Hart)
You Don't Know What Love Is (Gene DePaul and Don Raye)
You Took Advantage Of Me (Richard Rodgers and Lorenz Hart)

CHAPTER FIVE

PLAYING THE MELODY I

You should by now be fairly fluent at playing standard progressions that contain both primary and secondary jazz chords, and used the accompaniment models from the previous chapter. In this chapter, we shall learn how to play the melody and chords together. We shall adopt two alternative approaches: firstly a **shorthand** approach that makes a simple but effective arrangement of a song, and secondly a **longhand** approach that adheres more closely to voice-leading principles, and will provide the basis for a richer and more complex harmony.

THE SHORTHAND APPROACH

We have already observed that accompanying chords generally sound best when played just below the melodic line, this becomes crucial when playing the melody and chords together.

In the following example, the first eight bars of Victor Young and Ned Washington's "Stella by Starlight" are shown. The melodic line and voicing that lies immediately below it is played in the **right-hand**, accompanied by single bass notes in the **left-hand**. This we shall refer to as the "shorthand" approach:

Figure 5-1

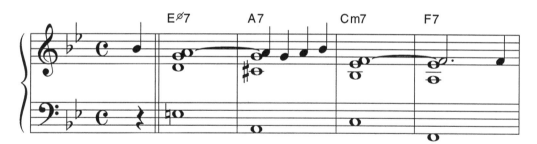

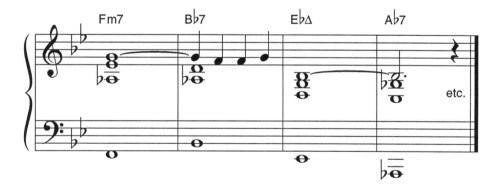

The register of the bass line is rarely specified in chord progressions. To ensure that each chord sounds evenly balanced and sonorous, a good rule of thumb is to play the bass note either a *seventh* or a *tenth* below the bottom note of each chord:

Figure 5-2

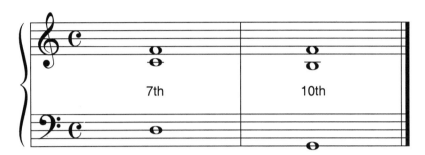

DOUBLING AND MERGING

Notes will often be the same in both the melody and the harmony. Wherever this occurs, the melody note can either **double** at the octave (appear as the melody note in one octave and as a harmony note in another), or **merge** and be played as a unison (coincide as one note).

In the following example, the first four bars of Neil Hefti's "Girl Talk" are shown. The melody note (G) begins as the third of E♭• and becomes the seventh of A7 ⌐n the third beat. It is also the third of E♭• and the seventh of A7 and **doubles** and octave lower than the melody to provide a balanced and sonorous accompaniment to the melody. On the other hand, in the second bar, the melody note (E♭) is also the seventh of Fm7 on the third beat and **merges** into a unison at this lower register:

Figure 5-3

Please note the following:

• Occasions for doubling or merging will usually be determined by the register of the melody. When the melody is in a high register, the doubling of the third or seventh at the octave can help spread the chord more evenly across the keyboard. When the melody is in a low register (around or below middle C), the merging of melody and harmony notes is preferable since doubling them would push the chords too low down the keyboard.

• Should the melodic line dip below the register of the chord after the chord has sounded, the sustaining pedal can be used to mask any breaks in the harmonic line. In the first bar of Richard A Whiting, Newell Chase and Leo Robin's "My Ideal", the melodic line dips below the voicings chosen for Eb∆, and again at the end of the second and third bar. In each case, the **sustaining pedal** can be used to mask any unavoidable breaks in the harmonic line:

Figure 5-4

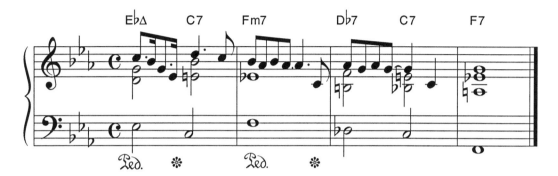

Conclusion:

The **shorthand** approach is achieved by selecting voicings that lie immediately below each melody note in the right-hand and follows the contour of the melodic line. Depending on the register of the melodic line, the melody notes may double or merge with harmony notes, resulting in a simple but effective arrangement of a song, one that clearly defines the melody and harmony.

PROCEDURE

a) Select a standard song and learn to play the melodic line from memory.

b) Play the melody and the bass notes (as indicated by the chord symbols) from memory.

c) Play through the chord progression in three-parts while singing or humming the melody, referring to the accompaniment models in the previous chapter.

d) Make an arrangement of the song using the shorthand approach shown above.

Useful Tip:

The following method may prove useful for finding the correct voicing:

• Firstly, find the **melody** note.

• Secondly, find the **bass** note.

• Thirdly, find the **voicing** of the chord that lies immediately below the melody note in the right-hand.

THE LONGHAND APPROACH

One of the joys of playing jazz piano is being able to choose from a wealth of harmonic possibilities to elaborate an otherwise plain chord progression. We shall learn more about this process in **Part Two**, but for now we must lay the foundations for a richer harmonic language, by reintroducing the voice-leading principle from *Chapter Three*. We shall begin by spreading the chord across both hands to produce an alternative melodic accompaniment.

In the following example, an alternative arrangement of "Stella By Starlight" is shown, this time spreading the chords evenly across both hands:

Figure 5-5

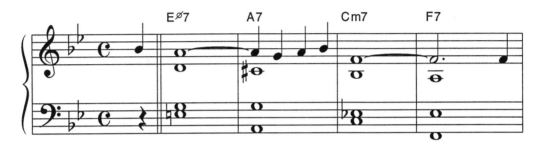

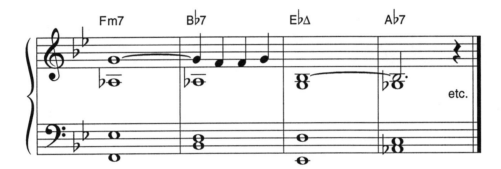

Please note the following:

• Compare the above arrangement with the **Figure 5-1**. Throughout the previous example, the third and seventh proceed to the nearest inversion of each subsequent chord.

• The above arrangement may sound less balanced due to the lower register of the chords and the larger spaces that now appear between the melody and chords, but it provides the basis for a richer harmonic language, one where a fourth and fifth part can be introduced at a later stage.

In the following example, the first eight bars of Victor Schwertzinger and Johnny Mercer's "Tangerine" are shown. A balanced arrangement is created by playing the chords with either the right-hand, or else spreading them across both hands. This we shall refer to as the **longhand** approach:

Figure 5-6

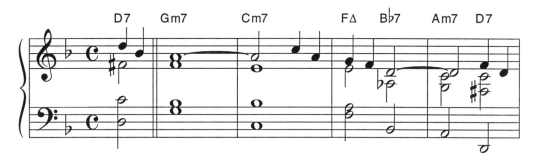

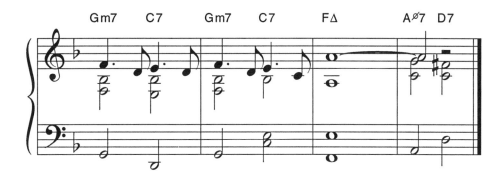

In bars 1 and 2, the chords are spread across both hands. When the melody dips to the lower register on the B♭7 chord (D), the third and seventh are taken into the right-hand until the second beat of bar 6. On the third beat of bar 6, the C7 chord is again spread across both hands in anticipation of the melodic leap (C to A) on the FΔ chord. Consequently, good voice-leading is maintained throughout.

Please note the following:

• The melody and chords can be played together using one of two approaches, either a *shorthand* approach, for an immediate and effective arrangement of a song; or a *longhand* approach that adheres more strictly to voice-leading principles and providing the basis for a richer harmonic language.

• Both approaches can be made easier to play by *rhythmically displacing* the chords or bass notes. Syncopations and repetitions of chords can also be introduced to provide harmonic motion during held notes and give the arrangements a stronger jazz feel.

• Remember that the better the chords have been learned in three parts, the easier it will be to play them when the melody is added.

AN APPROACH FOR SMALL AND LARGE HANDS

Learning a song will inevitably involve overcoming difficulties that do not fall neatly into our harmonic system, such as unusual chord symbols, melodic leaps and rhythmic displacements. It is the continual process of overcoming these difficulties, as well as becoming increasingly familiar with the language of jazz chord progressions, that will give us the skill and fluidity needed to improvise elaborate arrangements in a broad range of jazz styles.

Before we consider some of these difficulties, we should explode a common myth:

"You need to have large hands to play jazz piano!"

Though it is true that the size of a pianist's hands may dictate how he or she approaches certain aspects of piano playing, particularly in jazz where the exact placement of chords is rarely specified. This is not a qualitative judgement but rather an observation of style. Nevertheless, it is advantageous to be able to stretch a tenth in the left-hand - a sonority much favoured by solo jazz pianists. It is a sizeable stretch for most pianists, especially between black and white keys (E♭ to G, or E to G♯ etc.).

Only a pianist with large hands could comfortably play the left-hand tenth on the Fm7 chord shown here. A tenth also appears in the second bar, though this time the melody and the chord are both played in the right-hand, making the left-hand stretch unnecessary:

Figure 5-7

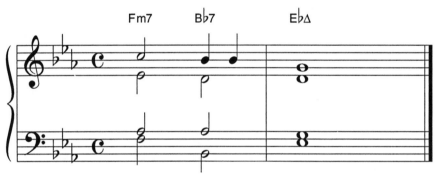

An alternative arrangement could be made by playing the bass note up an octave on the first and last chord, thereby placing all the notes within the stretch of a pianist with smaller hands. This makes for a lighter and more "delicate" arrangement of the same melodic extract:

Figure 5-8

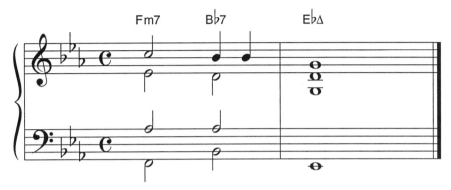

RHYTHMIC DISPLACEMENT OF THE CHORDS

The limitations placed on pianists with small hands can be mostly overcome by **rhythmically displacing** either the chord or bass note. In the following example, the chord Fm7 is delayed to the second beat of the bar, while the sustaining pedal is used to mask the break in the harmonic line:

Figure 5-9

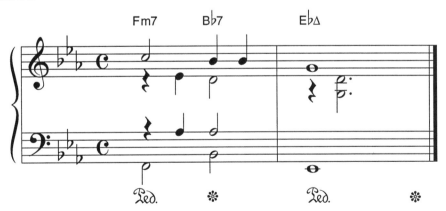

Alternatively, the rhythm of the bass could be rhythmically delayed to the second beat:

Figure 5-10

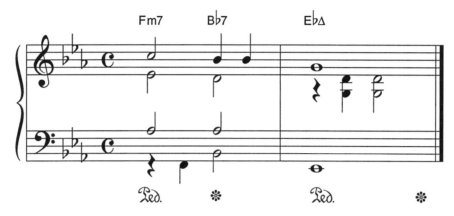

The displaced chord shown in **Figure 5-8** could also have been played entirely by the left-hand, again the sustaining pedal is used to mask the break in the harmonic line:

Figure 5-11

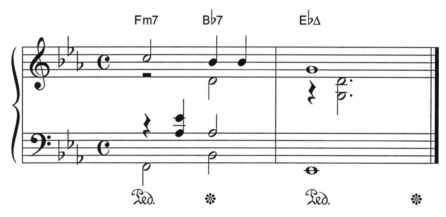

Alternatively, the delayed chord in the first bar could be played by the right-hand:

Figure 5-12

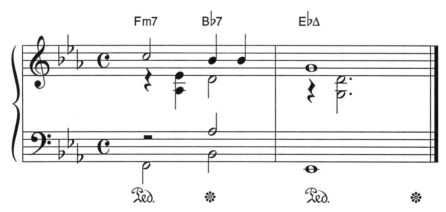

Please note the following:

• Rhythmically displacing either the chord or bass note is a practical and effective way of playing notes that are normally out of reach.

• A skilled jazz pianist should be able to move freely from spreading the chords across both hands to playing them entirely in the left-hand or right-hand.

• Rhythmic displacement also introduces a degree of **harmonic motion**: this is particularly effective during long and held notes, where the melody is momentarily static and some motion in the accompaniment is desirable.

• At this stage, the third and seventh should always be played **simultaneously**, no matter how they are spread across the hands. Aim for a crisp and precise harmonic accompaniment to the melody by resisting the temptation to stagger the third and seventh.

• At this stage, the melody should be played as accurately as possible, limiting rhythmic displacement to the accompanying chords and bass notes.

HANDLING LEAPS

There will be occasions when it is desirable to play the melody in the right-hand accompanied by the bass notes and chords in the left-hand. This is particularly practical when the register of the melody is constantly changing, as is often the case in a waltz.

In a waltz, the bass note is customarily played on the first beat of each bar, then the chord is played and held for the second and third beat. The result is a form of stride piano in 3/4 time, involving constant leaps between the bass notes and chords.

In the following example, the first four bars of Henry Mancini and Johnny Mercer's "Moon River" are shown. The left-hand accompaniment **leaps** between the bass notes and chords:

Figure 5-13

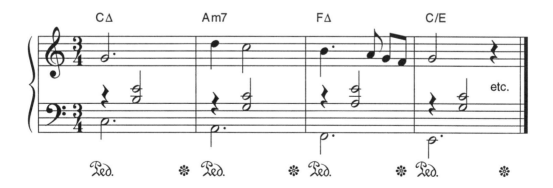

The bass notes can also be played in a very low register, taking full advantage of the piano's deepest sonorities:

Figure 5-14

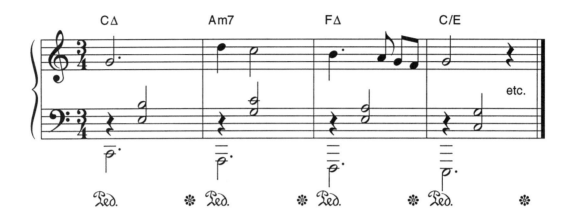

THE VOICING SHIFT

There will often be times when the melody dramatically changes register, sometimes by more than an octave. In such cases the accompaniment will also need to change register.

In the third bar of Richard Himber and Stuart Allen "If I Should Lose You," the register of the melody suddenly rises by an octave, consequently it is accompanied by a **shift** in the register of the chords:

Figure 5-15

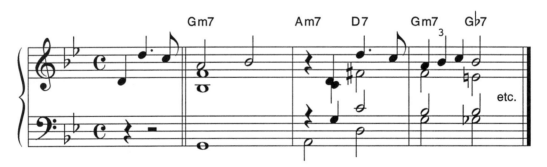

Please note the following:

• Exactly where a voicing shift is needed will depend on the particular contour of the melody, as well as the size of the pianist's hands.

• The sustaining pedal can be used to mask any undesirable breaks in the harmonic line.

• Changes of register can also be introduced for dramatic effect. For example: the melody can be transposed up an octave for a couple of bars and then return to its original register.

RHYTHMIC INTEREST

Having displaced the rhythm of the chordal accompaniment, more elaborate repetitions and syncopations can be introduced to create a stronger **jazz feel**. This can be done most effectively during held notes, when there is sufficient time and space for the accompanying chords to be heard, and it is desirable to have some motion in the accompaniment.

The first eight bars of John Green and Edward Heyman's "Out Of Nowhere" contains several held notes, the chords are repeated or syncopated to create motion in the accompaniment:

Figure 5-16

Exercises:

i) Select a standard song and make a **shorthand** version, using the procedures outlined in this chapter.

ii) Select the same song and make a **longhand** version, spreading the chords across the two hands wherever necessary to maintain good voice-leading throughout the arrangement.

iii) Displace the rhythm of both the chords and bass notes to enhance the arrangement, before introducing some rhythmic interest during the held notes to create a stronger jazz feel.

CHAPTER SIX

BASIC JAZZ THEORY

In this chapter, we shall examine the theory behind the progressions we have been playing. We shall begin by constructing **triads** and **seventh chords** on each degree of the major scale, and learn about **V-I** and **II-V-I cadences**, the **cycle of fifths** and **turnarounds**.

TRIADS

Triads are the building blocks of Western music and can be played on any degree of the major scale. Classical theory refers to triads I, IV and V as the **tonal** degrees (major), triads III and VI as the **modal** degrees (minor), triad II as either **tonal** or **modal** depending on its harmonic function (major or minor), and triad VII as the **leading-tone** triad (diminished).

These triads are related because they are all present in the C major scale:

Figure 6-1

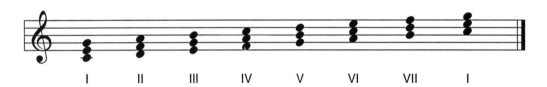

The harmonic importance of the **tonal** degree triads (I, IV, and V) cannot be overstated: they form the **axis** of tonal harmony. In the key of C major, chord V (G major) is situated a perfect fifth *above* the tonic, while chord IV (F major) is situated a perfect fifth *below* the tonic, the tonic triad is equidistant between the two other triads. Triads I, IV and V are the only triads required to harmonise a melody consisting of notes found in the major scale.

In the following example, each note of the C major scale is shown harmonised by one or more of the tonal degree triads (I, IV and V):

Figure 6-2

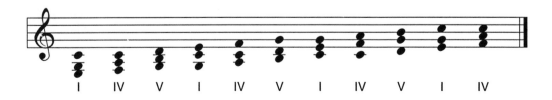

SEVENTH CHORDS

Seventh chords can also be played on each degree of the major scale:

Figure 6-3

THE V-I CADENCE

A cadence is defined as a succession of two or more chords that pertain to the conclusion of a musical phrase. The most conclusive and important cadence is the **V-I** or **perfect cadence** and is a succession from chords V to I in any given key (jazz theory refers to a V-I cadence whereas classical theory refers to a perfect cadence).

The V chord is referred to as the **dominant** due to its crucial function in the perfect cadence. A minor seventh interval can be added to the dominant chord to make a more emphatic sounding cadence. This chord is then referred to as a **dominant seventh** chord.

In the following example, a V-I cadence in C major is shown. Notice how the **dissonance** between the third and seventh **resolves** to the tonic and third in the subsequent chord:

Figure 6-4

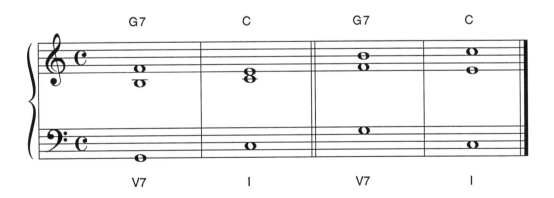

THE II-V-I CADENCE

The V-I cadence can also be extended to include the chord built on the V of the V.

In the key of C major, if C is the I (tonic), G is the V (dominant), the chord built on the V of the V (the V of G) must be a D chord. This new chord must be a **minor seventh** chord to be in the key of C major. The result is a succession of three chords in the same key: the first is a minor seventh chord, the second is a dominant seventh chord, the third is a major seventh chord. Collectively, they are referred to as a **II-V-I Cadence**:

Figure 6-5

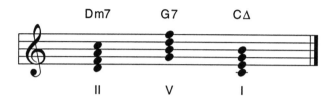

The cadence can also be shown in three-part harmony:

Figure 6-6

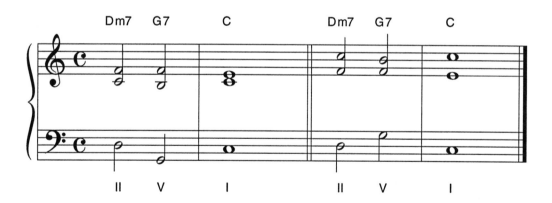

THE II-V-I CADENCE IN THE MINOR KEY

The II-V-I cadence in the minor key but will need the following adjustments:

• The II chord must include a **diminished fifth** in accordance with the key signature.

• The V chord will remain **major** despite being in the minor key, and will need an **accidental**.

• The I chord will be **minor**.

Figure 6-7

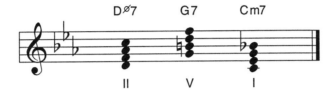

The cadence can also be shown in three-part harmony:

Figure 6-8

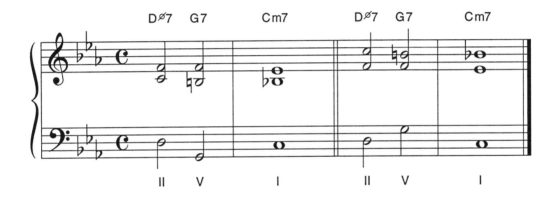

Summary

The II-V-I cadences consist of the following:

II - a minor seventh chord in a major II-V-I cadence; a half-diminished seventh chord in a minor II-V-I cadence.

V - a dominant seventh chord (seventh chord) in both a major or minor II-V-I cadence.

I - a major seventh or sixth chord in a major II-V-I cadence; a minor seventh or sixth chord in a minor II-V-I cadence.

• It is useful to be familiar with **roman** as well as **jazz chord notation**. The advantage of roman numerals is that underlying harmonic structures can be clearly seen, making it easier to transpose chord progressions.

• **New roman** can be used when indicating minor chords. For example: ii-V-I.

HARMONIC STRUCTURE AND FORM

Major and minor II-V-I cadences provide the underlying harmonic structure of most standard chord progressions. Standard songs typically consist of a succession of II-V-I cadences that are constantly being interrupted and modulating into other keys.

Outlined below is the harmonic structure of Hoagy Carmichael and Ned Washington's "The Nearness Of You". The first example shows the chord progression using jazz chord notation, the second uses roman numerals:

Example 6-1

‖   E♭Δ | B♭m7   E♭7 | A♭m7 | A♭°7 |

| Gm7   C7 | Fm7   B♭7 | Gm7   C7 | Fm7   B♭7 ‖

‖   E♭Δ | B♭m7   E♭7 | A♭m7 | A♭°7 |

| Gm7   C7 | Fm7   B♭7 | E♭Δ   A♭7 | E♭Δ   ‖

‖   Fm7 | B♭7 | E♭Δ   E♭7 | B♭m7   E♭7 |

| A♭Δ   Aø7   D7 | Gm7   C7 | F7 | Fm7   B♭7 ‖

‖   E♭Δ | B♭m7   E♭7 | A♭m7 | A♭°7 |

| Gm7   C7 | Fm7   B♭7 | Gø7 | C7 |

| Fm7 | B♭7 | E♭6 | ‘⁄.   ‖

Example 6-2

‖ E♭:   I | A♭: ii   V | I | I   I(dim) |

| E♭: iii   VI | ii   V | iii   VI | ii   V |

‖ E♭:   I | A♭: ii   V | I | I   I(dim) |

| E♭: iii   VI | ii   V | I   VI | ii   V   ‖

‖ E♭:   ii | V | I | A♭: ii   V |

| | Gm: ii V | I   F: V | I | | E♭: ii   V   ‖

‖ E♭:   I | A♭: ii   V | I | I   I(dim) |

| E♭: iii   VI | ii   V | Fm: ii | V |

| E♭:   ii | V | I | I   '/.   ‖

A-A-B-A FORM

The form of "The Nearness Of You" is **A-A-B-A + coda**. Each section consists of eight bars, the first is referred to as the **A** section and is immediately repeated (but with different words). This is then followed by the **B** section which passes through other keys and can be referred to as the **middle eight**, **bridge** or **release**. The **A** section is then repeated followed by a four bar **coda**, sometimes referred to as a **tag** ending.

Example 6-4:

‖ **A** (8 bars) | **A** (8 bars) ‖ **B** (8 bars) ‖ **A** (8 bars) ‖ **(coda)** ‖

A-B FORM

An alternative **form** is **A-B** and it consists of two 8 or 16-bar sections. The second section usually begins as a repetition of the first but ends differently, sometimes with a coda ending:

Example 6-3:

‖   **A** (16 bars) | **B** (16 bars)   ‖

Please note the following:

• Most standards are based on one of the above forms.

• Not all standards include coda endings. In some cases the coda may only be played on the final rendition of the theme - this is most likely to occur in instrumental compositions.

• Where a standard does not fall into one of these categories, it will most likely be divided into either four, eight, twelve or sixteen bar sections.

THE CYCLE OF FIFTHS

Having understood the V-I and II-V-I cadence, and the principle by which a chord can be preceded by its dominant, the process can be linked into a sequence passing through all twelve keys, each chord functioning as the dominant of the next chord. It is referred to as the **cycle of fifths**.

It can be most clearly shown in the form of a circle: beginning with C at twelve o'clock, and then moving clockwise: C is the dominant (V) of F; F is the dominant (V) of Bb; Bb is the dominant (V) of Eb etc:

Example 6-5

The Cycle of Fifths:

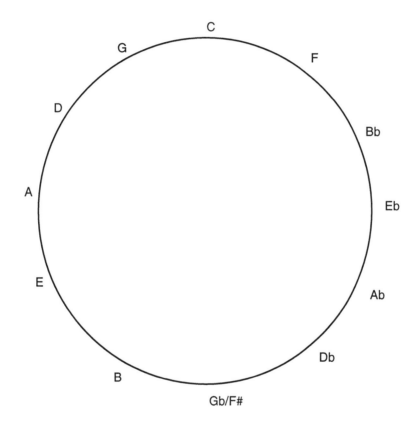

The cycle of fifths also coincides with the order in which **key signatures** are tabulated:

Flats:

Beginning with C, which has no flats or sharps, moving **clockwise** F has **one** flat, Bb has **two** flats, Eb has **three** flats etc.

Sharps:

Beginning with C, which has no flats or sharps, moving **counter-clockwise** G has **one** sharp, D has **two** sharps, A has **three** sharps etc.

THE CYCLE OF FIFTHS FOR THREE-PART CHORDS

Here is the start of the cycle for seventh, minor seventh and major seventh chords:

Figure 6-9

Dominant Seventh chords through the cycle of fifths:

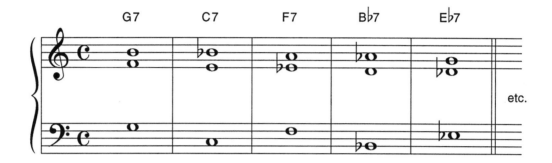

Figure 6-10

Minor Seventh chords through the cycle of fifths:

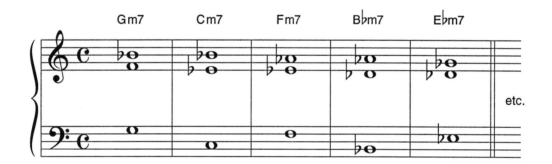

Figure 6-11

Major Seventh chords through the cycle of fifths:

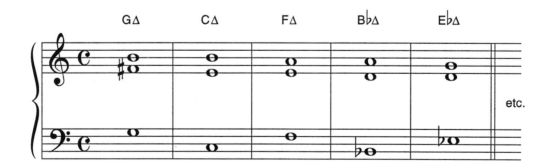

Please note the following:

• The cycle of fifths is sometimes referred to as the **circle of fifths**, the **cycle of fourths** or the **circle of fourths**. They all refer to the same thing, depending on whether the cycle is seen as moving in a clockwise or counter-clockwise direction.

• Remember that playing the fifth above any note on the keyboard will result in the same note as playing the fourth below it. It will be necessary to go both up and down when playing the bass notes on the piano to avoid running off the end of the keyboard.

• The cycle of fifths is a crucial component of jazz harmony and must be thoroughly learned. Practice the cycle with dominant seventh, minor seventh and major seventh chords as shown in **Figures 6-10**, **6-11** and **6-12**, moving to the nearest voicing of each subsequent chord.

TURNAROUNDS

A **turnaround** is a generic term used to describe a succession of chords played for one of the following purposes:

a) To return to the beginning of a chord progression in a logical harmonic way after the last chord has been sounded.

b) To provide a smooth harmonic transition to a new section of a song.

Turnarounds are often written into chord charts, sometimes they are shown in brackets at the end of a song or section. Where they are not written, it is useful to know some of the more common turnarounds, so that they can be introduced and varied as and where necessary.

Common turnarounds from **tonic** (I) to **tonic** (I) are as follows:

1)

| I | I | vi | I | ii | V | II | I ... |

| I | C | Am7 | I | Dm7 | G7 | II | C ... |

2)

| I | I | ♭III | I | ♭VI | ♭II | II | I ... |

| I | C | E♭∆ | I | A♭∆ | D♭∆ | II | C ... |

3)

| I | I | VI | I | ♭VI | V | II | I ... |

| I | C | A7 | I | A♭13 | G+7#9 | II | C ... |

• Common turnarounds from the **tonic** (I) to the **supertonic** (II) are as follows:

1)

| I | I | **IV** | I | **iii** | **VI** | II | **ii** ... |

| I | C | FΔ | I | Em7 | A7 | II | Dm7 ... |

2)

| I | I | **VII** | I | **♭VII** | **VI** | II | **ii** ... |

| I | C | B7 | I | B♭7 | A7 | II | Dm7 ... |

• Common turnarounds from the **tonic** (I) to the **subdominant** (IV) are as follows:

1)

| I | I | **vi** | **♭vi** | I | **v** | I | II | **IV** ... |

| I | C | Am7 | A♭m7 | I | Gm7 | C7 | II | F ... |

2)

| I | I | **ii** | I | **#ii°** | **Ic** | II | **IV** ... |

| I | C | Dm7 | I | D#°7 | C7/G | II | F ... |

• Common turnarounds from the **tonic** (I) to the **dominant** (V) are as follows:

1)

I	I	♭VII	I	vi	II	II	V ...

I	C	B♭7	I	Am7	D7	II	G ...

2)

I	I	#iº	I	IIsus	II	II	V ...

I	C	C#º7	I	D7sus	D7	II	G ...

Please note the following:

• There are many variations to the turnarounds shown here, but most of them refer to the cycle of fifths. Begin by learning these formulas and transpose them into other keys.

• Since many of these turnarounds can be found written in songbooks, their use and context should be quickly assimilated.

Exercises:

Select a key and form the following cadences, progressions and turnarounds:

i) V-I cadence in the major key

ii) V-I cadence in the minor key

iii) II-V-I cadence in the major key

iv) II-V-I cadence in the minor key

v) Play through the cycle of fifths beginning at any place using dominant seventh, minor seventh and then major seventh chords.

v) Select a key and construct turnarounds moving between the following chords:

 i) tonic to tonic

ii) tonic to supertonic

iii) tonic to subdominant

iv) tonic to dominant

PART TWO

In **Part One**, we learned about the rudiments of jazz harmony and how to make simple arrangements of standard songs. In **Part Two**, we shall introduce a more sophisticated harmonic language that will include chapters on: **reharmonization**, **five** and **six-part harmony**, **block chords**, **quartal** and **quintal harmony** as well as a chapter on the influence of **classical piano music** on jazz.

CHAPTER SEVEN

REHARMONIZATION I

One of the great joys of playing jazz piano is the scope for **reharmonization**. This is a process whereby a written chord progression can be modified to transform the way a melody sounds. The best approach is to introduce a series of clearly defined harmonic devices into the chord progressions we are playing. The devices shown here are divided into two groups: **Reharmonization I** concerns modifications to the right-hand voicing, **Reharmonization II** concerns modifications that include the left-hand bass note. We shall begin by reharmonizing each chord in a II-V-I cadence.

MINOR-MAJOR SEVENTH TO MINOR SEVENTH

Where a minor seventh chord is written (Dm7), a **minor-major seventh** chord can precede it (DmΔ). The **dissonance** of the major seventh interval **resolves** to the relative **consonance** of the minor seventh:

Figure 7-1

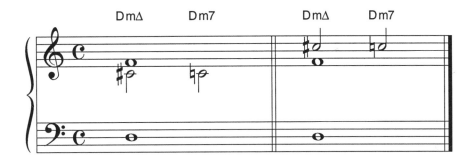

SUSPENDED FOURTH TO DOMINANT SEVENTH

Where a dominant seventh chord is written (G7), a **suspended fourth** chord can precede it (G7sus or G7sus4). The most widely used **suspension** occurs when the third of the chord is temporarily replaced by the fourth, before resolving down to the third:

Figure 7-2

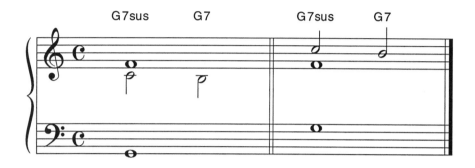

N.B. In classical theory, a suspension is defined as a tone whose natural progression has been rhythmically delayed. This would typically occur when moving between two triads with one of the notes in the first triad hanging over to the second before resolving to form the new triad.

MAJOR SEVENTH TO MAJOR SIXTH

Where a major seventh chord is written (I), the **major seventh** interval can fall to the **major sixth**. Since the major seventh interval is dissonant, its resolution to the major sixth is particularly effective at the end of a musical phrase:

Figure 7-3

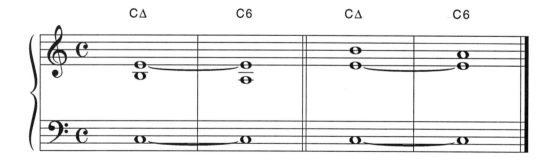

REHARMONIZATION AND THE II-V-I CADENCE

Having seen how each chord in a II-V-I cadence can be reharmonized, all three chords can now be shown together.

In the following example, a II-V-I cadence in C major is shown in its original form, and then with all three reharmonizations:

The original II-V-I cadence in C major shown in two registers:

Figure 7-4

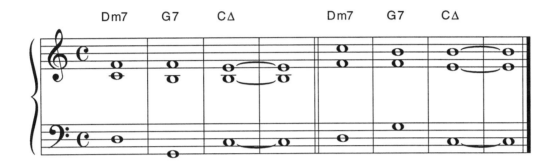

The same II-V-I cadence with reharmonization:

Figure 7-5

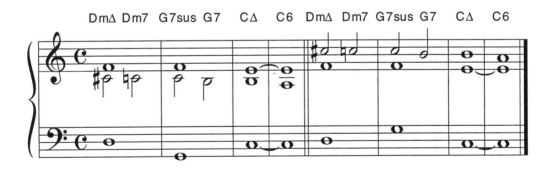

Alternatively, the minor-major seventh could *follow* the minor seventh chord in the first bar:

Figure 7-6

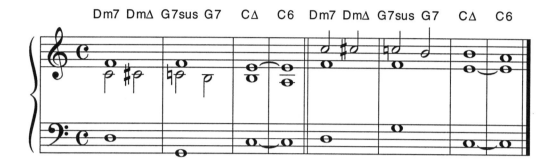

MAJOR SEVENTH TO DOMINANT SEVENTH

The **major seventh** chord can also precede the dominant seventh chord, creating a momentary dissonance. Though this harmonic device is less useful than the suspension, it can sound effective, particularly when more parts are added:

Figure 7-7

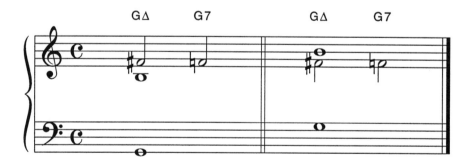

CHROMATIC SHIFTS

The dominant seventh chord can be approached by a **chromatic shift** either *upwards* or *downwards*. This device can be extended to any chord in the cadence, but is most effective when used when approaching the dominant seventh chord.

In the following example, the G7 chord is approached by a chromatic shift *upwards*:

Figure 7-8

In the following example, the G7 chord is approached by a chromatic shift *downwards*:

Figure 7-9

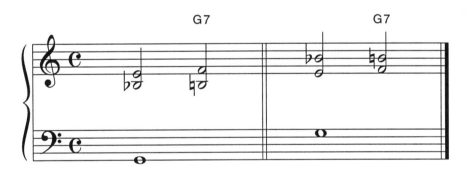

Please note the following:

• Reharmonizations sound most effective when there is sufficient time for them to be heard. If the harmonic rhythm of a chord progression is moving too fast, then subtle modifications to the harmony can be too cluttered to be musically satisfying.

• Reharmonizations sound particularly effective during pauses or breaks in the melodic line, where the increased movement in the harmony provides motion while the melody is static.

• It makes sense to become familiar with reharmonization within the context of three-part harmony before adding more parts or introducing a more complex harmonic language.

AVOIDING DISSONANCES

When playing the melody and chords together, special care must be taken to avoid playing harmony notes that are dissonant to the melody. This is most likely to occur when the melody note is also a harmony note, and any modifications to the harmony will create a dissonance.

In the following example, the melody begins on the third in the second bar, coinciding with the G7 chord. Introducing a suspension in this instance would clearly create a dissonance between the third in the melody and the suspension in the chord:

Figure 7-10

In the following example, the melody passes via the fifth and sixth in the second bar. In this instance, a suspension can be freely introduced to create some movement in the harmony without creating an undesirable dissonance between the melody and chords:

Figure 7-11

MUSICAL EXAMPLES

Shown here are some melodic extracts that demonstrate how reharmonization can enrich our arrangements of songs when playing the melody and chords together. As the progressions we are using consist mostly of II-V, V-I and II-V-I cadences, reharmonization can be used extensively.

The first eight bars of "Stella by Starlight" consist of two interrupted II-V cadences followed by a II-V-I cadence in E♭. The cadences are reharmonized without being dissonance to the melody:

Figure 7-12

In the ballad "It's Easy To Remember," a steady pulse is played, incorporating the same reharmonizations to create a counter-melody:

Figure 7-13

In the second bar of Sam Coslow and Arthur Johnson's "My Old Flame" the melody begins on an F♮, accompanied by a half-diminished seventh chord. A minor-major seventh is played here to create a particularly dissonant effect:

Figure 7-14

In Henry Mancini and Johnny Mercer's "Moon River," the harmonic rhythm remains constant throughout, by using reharmonization to ensure a note is played on each beat of the bar.

Figure 7-15

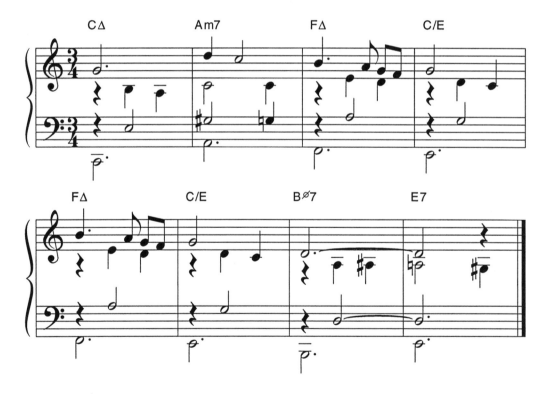

*N.B. An additional suspension is played in bars 4 and 6, from the **second** to the **tonic** (ninth to the tonic). In classical theory, any note of the triad can be suspended: from the second to tonic (2-1), from the fourth to the third (4-3), or from the sixth to the fifth (6-5).*

The melody of "Tangerine" begins with a II-V-I cadence in F, followed by a progression of chords through the cycle of fifths. The II-V-I cadence is reharmonized, while the fast moving chords that follow are unaltered:

Figure 7-16

The opening phrase of "My Ideal" can also be extensively reharmonized with the exception on the D♭7 chord, to introduce a suspension here would create a dissonance with the melody:

Figure 7-17

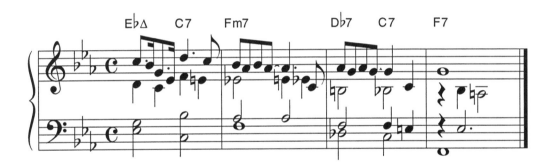

Finally, the first four bars of Johnny Green and Edward Heyman's "Out of Nowhere" are shown, this time with some rhythmic displacement of the chords. The first two bars alternate between major seventh and sixth chords to create some motion during the unchanging harmony:

Figure 7-18

PROCEDURE

The following procedure can be useful when practicing reharmonization:

a) Play through the chord progression of a song you know well.

b) Introduce **suspensions** on dominant seventh chords.

d) Introduce **minor-major sevenths** before or after minor seventh chords.

c) Resolve **major seventh** to **major sixth** chords.

e) Introduce **major sevenths** before dominant seventh chords as an alternative to suspensions.

f) Introduce **chromatic shifts** upwards or downwards to dominant seventh chords as well as other chords in the cadence as and where appropriate.

g) Introduce various combinations of the above reharmonizations, and practice them until the chord progression can be played smoothly at a steady tempo.

h) Play a balanced version of the chordal accompaniment that introduces reharmonizations as and where appropriate (sparingly) to enhance the melodic line.

i) Finally introduce the melody adopting either a **shorthand** or **longhand** approach, introducing reharmonization as and where appropriate. Take special care to avoid undesirable dissonances that may occur between the melody and chords.

Please note the following:

• Remember that reharmonizations sound most effective when the harmonic rhythm is sufficiently slow for them to be heard, where some harmonic motion is especially desirable. For example: during a pause or break in the melodic line.

• Remember that reharmonization is always **optional** and never compulsory. The best approach is to begin by exploring all harmonic variations before arriving at an arrangement of each song that uses reharmonization **sparingly** to enhance the melody.

REHARMONIZATION II

In **Reharmonization II**, we shall introduce modifications to the left-hand bass notes, including **tritone substitution** and **pedal notes**.

TRITONE SUBSTITUTION AND THE DOMINANT SEVENTH CHORD

Tritone substitution (flattened fifth or diminished fifth substitution) involves altering the bass note by a tritone or diminished fifth to create a new relationship with the right-hand voicing. We shall begin by introducing this reharmonization to the dominant seventh chord as part of a V-I cadence.

The V-I cadence in C major:

Figure 7-19

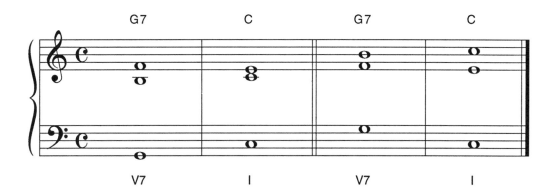

Q. In the above example, B is the major third and F is the minor seventh interval of the G7 chord. What is the interval between B and F?

A. It is a **tritone** (diminished fifth, flattened fifth or augmented fourth); the tritone is a unique interval since it divides the octave into two equal halves.

Q. Since B to F, and F to B are the same interval, it must follow that there is another dominant seventh chord for which B is the minor seventh interval and F is the third?

A. The answer is D♭7.

N.B. The term "tritone" is derived from the Greek; "tri-tone" meaning "three tones".

In the following example, the bass note (G) has been replaced by its tritone (Db). The G7 and Db7 chords are related since they share the same third and seventh. In jazz theory, the Db7 chord is referred to as the **tritone substitution** of G7:

Figure 7-20

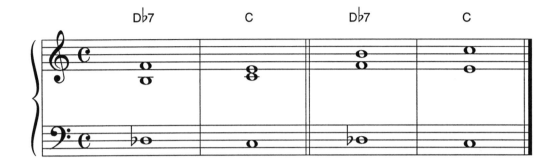

The tritone substitution chord can also inserted *between* the V and I of the cadence:

Figure 7-21

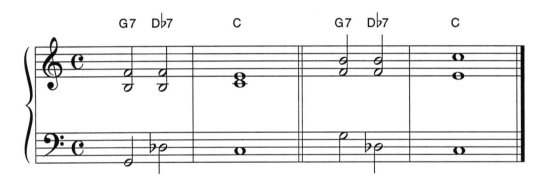

Tritone substitution can be practiced by applying it to each **dominant seventh** chord in the cycle of fifths:

Figure 7-22

Dominant Seventh chords through the cycle of fifths with tritone substitution:

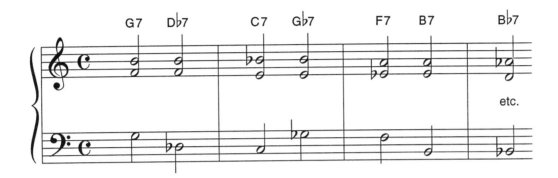

TRITONE SUBSTITUTION AND THE MINOR SEVENTH CHORD

Though tritone substitution is most commonly applied to dominant seventh chords as part of a V-I or II-V-I cadence or progression, it can also be applied to minor seventh and major seventh chords.

In the following example, the same bass line is played for **minor seventh** chords in the cycle of fifths, though the new chords formed by the altered bass note are not minor seventh but **major sixth** chords:

Figure 7-23

Minor Seventh chords through the cycle of fifths with tritone substitution:

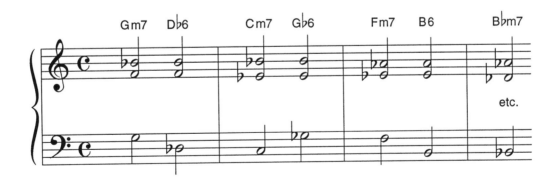

There is a variation for minor seventh chords that can be played provided it is followed by a dominant seventh chord (as in a II-V or II-V-I cadence), and does not create a dissonance with the melody. The right-hand voicing can be altered to form a **dominant seventh** chord on the tritone, which descends chromatically to form the next dominant seventh chord.

In the following example, the minor third interval is *raised* by a semitone to create a Db7 chord, before descending chromatically to form a C7 chord:

Figure 7-24

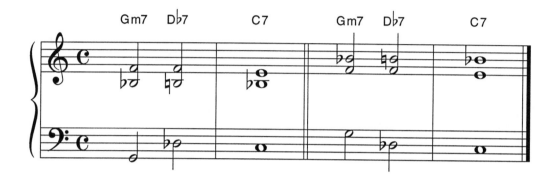

TRITONE SUBSTITUTION AND THE MAJOR SEVENTH CHORD

Finally, we shall apply tritone substitution to **major seventh** chords in exactly same way as for dominant seventh and minor seventh chords, though a chromatic adjustment will be needed for the substitution chord.

In the following example, the major seventh interval descends *chromatically* for each tritone substitution chord to produce a **dominant seventh** chord on the tritone. This is necessary because a mere repetition of the same chord would produce a suspended fourth chord on the tritone, which could not logically resolve onto the next chord in the cycle of fifths:

Figure 7-25

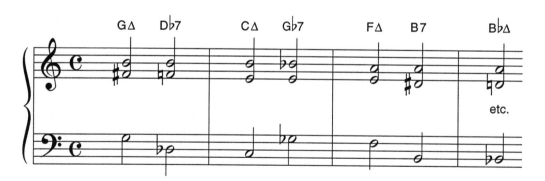

Exercise:

i) Practice the cycle of fifths with tritone substitution, beginning in any key until they become fluent (**Figures 7-20** to **7-23**).

SUBSTITUTION OF THE II-V ON THE TRITONE

Alternatively, the II-V of a II-V-I cadence could be replaced entirely by a II-V on the tritone, though such extreme reharmonization may often be dissonant with the melody.

In the following example the D♭7 chord, which is the tritone substitution chord of G7, is preceded by its II chord A♭m7, forming a II-V progression *on* the tritone:

Figure 7-26

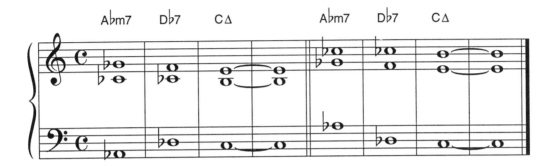

Please note the following:

• Tritone substitution as a reharmonization technique can be used extensively when playing a II-V or II-V-I cadence, or when moving between any two chords in the cycle of fifths.

• For the major seventh, minor seventh and dominant seventh chords, the tritone substitution chord can always be a **dominant seventh** chord, but for the minor seventh alone, there is an alternative substitution chord of a major sixth (**Figure 7-21**).

• The right-hand reharmonizations shown in the first half of this chapter cannot be combined with tritone substitution. For example: it is not practical to include a suspension in a tritone substitution of a dominant seventh chord.

• The melody invariably suggests which reharmonizations are most likely to be effective, and which are too dissonant to be musically desirable.

MUSICAL EXAMPLES

Shown here are some more melodic extracts, this time demonstrating how tritone substitution can be introduced to enhance our arrangements of standard songs. Notice how the chords are often spread across both hands, providing a smooth accompaniment for the melody.

In the first example, the first four bars of "It's Easy to Remember" are accompanied using tritone substitution chords on the second and fourth beats. Notice also that an additional passing note is introduced in the bass on the second beat of bar 2 (E♭-D), maintaining the harmonic rhythm during the pause in the melody, as well as providing a smooth transition between the E♭∆ and the C7 chord:

Figure 7-27

The first four bars of Ray Evans and Jay Livingston's "Never Let Me Go" begins with a II-V-I cadence in B♭. A tritone substitution chord is inserted on the last beat of bars 2 and 3 immediately before each new chord. A suspension is also introduced on the dominant seventh chord (C7):

Figure 7-28

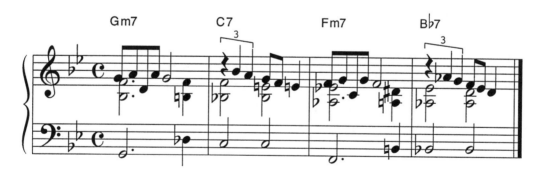

The first two bars of "Girl Talk" feature two major seventh chords on the cycle of fifths (Eb△-Ab△). Most songbooks include a tritone substitution chord between the two chords (A7):

Figure 7-29

The opening six bars of Ralph Rainger and Leo Robin's "If I Should Lose You" include a II-V-I cadences in both G minor and Eb major. In each case, the dominant seventh chord is replaced entirely by its tritone substitution chord. This is done by simply changing the bass note to the tritone:

Figure 7-30

The first two bars of "Tangerine" can also be transformed by introducing a tritone substitution chord between the II, the V and I of the II-V-I cadence in F. Notice that the chord second chord in bar two is delayed to the last beat to make it easier to stretch in the right-hand:

Figure 7-31

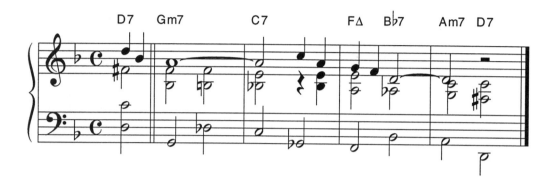

Finally, tritone substitution can be combined with rhythmic displacement. In the first four bars of Sammy Fain, Irving Kahal and Pierre Norman's "You Brought a New Kind of Love to Me," tritone substitution chords accompany the held note notes at the end of bars 1 and 2:

Figure 7-32

THE PEDAL NOTE

A **pedal note** or **pedal point** can be defined as "a tone that persists in one voice throughout several changes of harmony." Its most likely appearance is in the bass, where the same bass note can underlie several chords in a progression. An effective application of this device is to play a II-V or II-V-I cadence over a **dominant** pedal.

In the following example, Dm7 is played over a dominant pedal (G). The resulting Dm7/G chord is the same as a suspension of the V chord (G7sus), this is then followed by its resolution (G7):

Figure 7-33

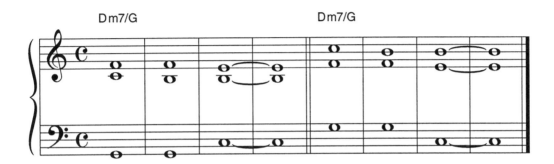

In the following example, the dominant pedal is extended to include all three chords in the cadence, the final chord being a second inversion chord of the tonic (CΔ/G):

Figure 7-34

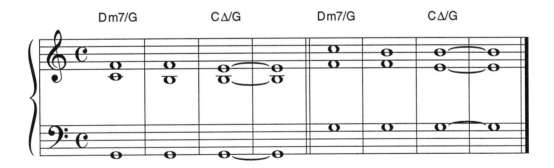

The dominant pedal can also be combined with the right-hand reharmonizations shown at the beginning of this chapter:

Figure 7-35

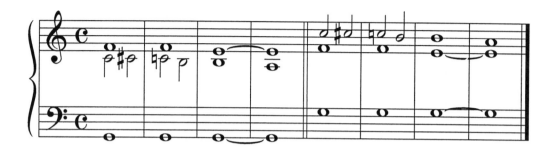

Finally, the dominant pedal can be played under more chords derived from the cycle of fifths. In the following example, the II-V-I cadence is preceded by an additional II-V progression, resulting in a III-VI-II-V cadence played over the dominant pedal:

Figure 7-36

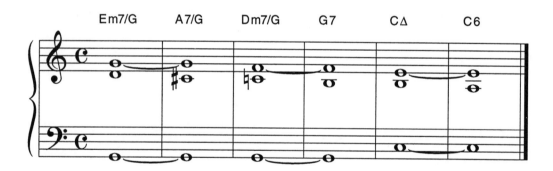

Please note the following:

• Pedal notes can be found in many different musical styles and idioms, particularly in Eastern and Indian music. However, the application shown here is most similar to that found in the Baroque music of J. S. Bach and G. F. Handel.

• Pedal notes are a most effective way of creating tranquillity and static tension in otherwise fast moving chord progressions. For example, the first for bars of Richard Rodgers and Lorenz Hart's "It's Easy To Remember" consists of two II-V-I cadences in E♭ major, bridged by a dominant seventh chord on the third beat of the second bar (C7). Both cadences can be played over a dominant pedal (B♭) to create a degree of tranquillity and static tension:

Example 7-1

‖ Fm7/B♭   B♭7 | E♭/B♭   C7/B♭ | Fm7/B♭   B♭7 | E♭△/B♭   ‖

Figure 7-37

Conclusion:

Though it will take some time to become fully conversant with the reharmonization procedures shown in this chapter, their usage will greatly enhance your musical vocabulary. Be sure to fully understand each procedure before introducing them into songs, and remember that reharmonization is always **optional** rather than compulsory. It will be most effective when used sparingly and where the harmonic rhythm is sufficiently slow for the new harmonic relationships to be fully heard and appreciated.

CHAPTER EIGHT

FOUR-PART HARMONY

Until now, all chord progressions have been played in three parts. In this chapter, a **fourth part** will be added, giving each chord more substance and harmonic richness. As we shall see, voice-leading principles will continue to be crucial, particularly when reharmonizing the chord progressions shown in *Chapter Seven*.

EXTENSIONS FOR PRIMARY JAZZ CHORDS

The term **extension** refers to those intervals that lie above the chord base (tonic, third, fifth, seventh). Shown above the octave they are as follows:

Figure 8-1

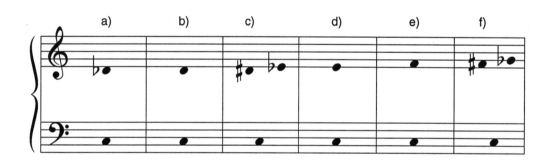

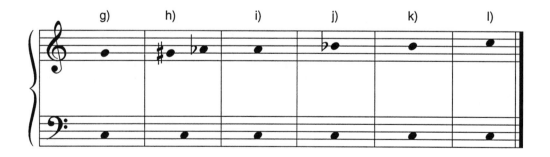

Key:

a) flattened ninth
b) ninth
c) sharpened ninth (minor tenth)
d) octave + third (major tenth)
e) eleventh
f) sharpened eleventh
g) octave + fifth
h) flattened thirteenth
i) thirteenth
j) octave + minor seventh
k) octave + major seventh
l) two octaves

Please note the following:

• The octave + fifth and the octave + seventh do not require further description, since they are already present in the chord base.

• The octave + third can also be referred to as a major or minor **tenth**.

EXTENSIONS FOR THE DOMINANT SEVENTH CHORD

Ten of the above extension intervals can be played above the **dominant seventh** chord base without sounding too dissonant. Here they are shown in two groups of five voicings, with the extension interval lying immediately above the chord base:

Figure 8-2

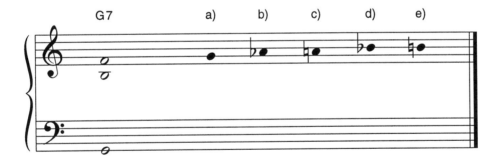

Key:

a) octave
b) ♭9
c) 9
d) ♯9 or +9
e) major tenth (doubling of major third)

Figure 8-3

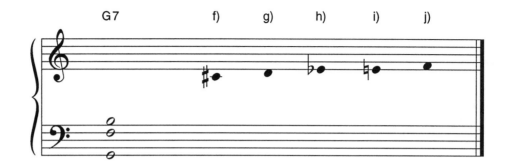

Key:

f) ♯4, +4, ♭5, ♯11 or +11
g) fifth
h) aug, +, +5, or ♭13
i) 6 or 13
j) doubling of minor seventh

Please note the following:

• Each voicing suggests a **harmonic colour** and easy to play with the right-hand.

• Of the twelve notes in the chromatic scale, ten can be played as extension intervals for dominant seventh chords. The two intervals that are not shown are the **perfect fourth** and **major seventh** (C and F# in the G7 chord), these intervals are too dissonant to be effective in this musical context.

• No matter which extension interval is played above the chord base, it will remain a dominant seventh chord.

• At this stage, all extension intervals should be played **above** the chord base.

• They can also be referred to as **auxiliary** intervals.

• There is no standard way of symbolising extension intervals, rather a variety of notational systems are in use, all can easily be deciphered. For example: "+" is often used for "♯", while "-" is used for "♭".

Symbolizing extensions:

Extension intervals generally appear slightly raised after each chord name:

Figure 8-4

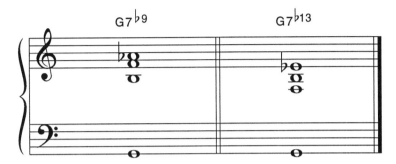

Chords with the tonic, third, fifth, or seventh (chord tones) as an extension interval are not generally symbolized:

Figure 8-5

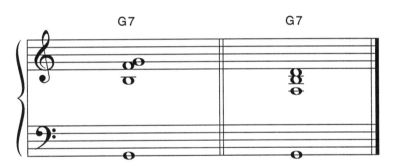

EXTENSIONS FOR THE MAJOR SEVENTH CHORD

We have seen that there is a choice of ten extension intervals for dominant seventh chords. The same freedom cannot be extended to major seventh chords, as several extensions will sound extremely dissonant. In order to begin the process of building a fourth line *above* three-part chord progressions, we must introduce the following restriction:

Restriction:

• The **fifth** and **ninth** are the only extension intervals that can be played above **major seventh** chords, according to which voicing is played:

Figure 8-6

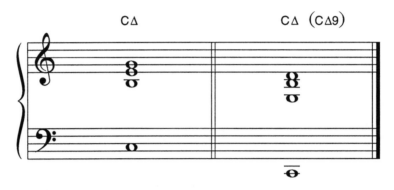

EXTENSIONS FOR THE MINOR SEVENTH CHORD

The same restriction must be applied to the minor seventh chord:

Restriction:

The **fifth** and **ninth** are the only extension intervals that can be played above **minor seventh** chords, according to which voicing is played:

Figure 8-7

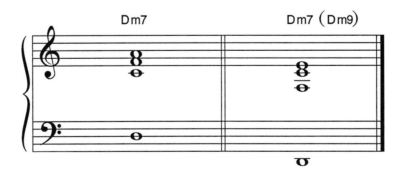

EXTENSIONS FOR THE HALF-DIMINISHED SEVENTH CHORD

For the **half-diminished seventh**, the fifth must be **flattened**. Exceptionally, we shall let the flattened fifth be played *below* the seventh and third as an alternative to the more strident sounding ninth:

Figure 8-8

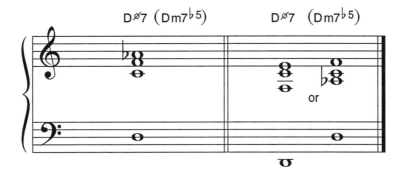

EXTENSIONS FOR THE DIMINISHED SEVENTH CHORD

For the **diminished seventh**, the fourth part should be the next available interval chord tone above the chord base:

Figure 8-9:

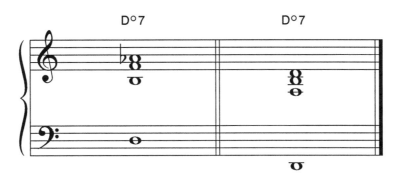

Please note the following:

• The voicings shown for major seventh, minor seventh, diminished and half-diminished seventh chords does not include all the harmonic possibilities, but restricting our options at this stage will help us to build logical four-part chord progressions.

• With the exception of the alternative half-diminished seventh chord shown in **Figure 8-8**, all extension intervals should be played *above* the three-part chord base.

• The chords shown here are identical to those played on the guitar in **bossa nova** music.

II-V-I CADENCES IN FOUR PARTS

To apply this knowledge to chord progressions, we shall begin by building a **fourth line** above the II-V-I cadence.

In the following example, the **fifth** above the minor seventh chord descends chromatically to form the **flattened ninth** above the dominant seventh chord, and subsequently descends chromatically to form the **fifth** above the major seventh chord:

Figure 8-10

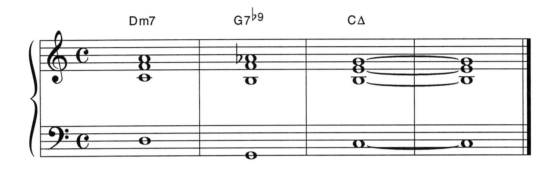

In the following example, the **ninth** above the minor seventh chord descends chromatically to form the **flattened thirteenth** above the dominant seventh chord, and subsequently descends chromatically to form the **ninth** above the major seventh chord:

Figure 8-11

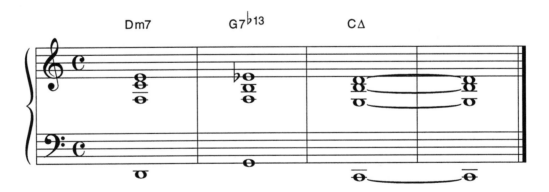

The dominant seventh chord could have included any one of the extension intervals shown in **Figures 8-2** and **8-3**, though by descending chromatically via the flattened ninth and the flattened thirteenth respectively, a **smooth harmonic line** was created.

Alternatively, the fourth part can descend duration of the dominant seventh chord. This is an effective way of introducing some harmonic motion, and drawing attention to the harmonic line or **counter-melody** created by the fourth part:

Figure 8-12

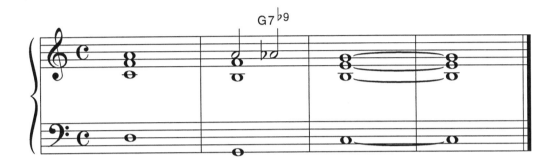

or alternatively:

Figure 8-13

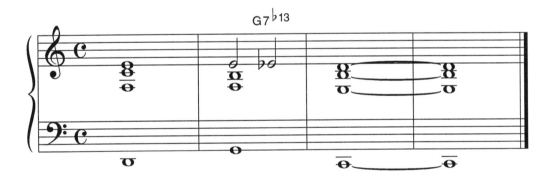

Exercises:

i) Play a dominant seventh, major seventh, minor seventh, half-diminished or diminished chord in any key and find appropriate extension interval(s).

ii) Having played a four-part chord in one voicing, find the alternative voicing changing the extension interval as necessary.

iii) Practice playing II-V-I cadences in all keys using the chord progressions shown in **Figures 8-9**, **8-10**, **8-11** and **8-12**.

iv) Practice playing the II-V-I cadences using the following key patterns:

a) Moving through the **cycle of fifths**:

$\parallel$ Dm7   G7   CΔ $\parallel$ Cm7   F7   B$\flat\Delta$ $\parallel$ B$\flat$m7   E$\flat$7   A$\flat\Delta$ $\parallel$ etc.

b) Ascending **chromatically**:

$\parallel$ Dm7   G7   CΔ $\parallel$ E$\flat$m7   A$\flat$7   D$\flat\Delta$ $\parallel$ Em7   A7   DΔ $\parallel$ etc.

c) Descending **chromatically**:

$\parallel$ Dm7   G7   CΔ $\parallel$ C$\sharp$m7   F$\sharp$7   BΔ $\parallel$ Cm7   F7   B$\flat\Delta$ $\parallel$ etc.

MINOR II-V-I CADENCES IN FOUR PARTS

To add a fourth line above a **minor** II-V-I cadence, the fifth must be flattened on the minor seventh chord [II]. The ninth can be played In the alternative voicing, this can sound effective, particularly if the melody note above the chord is the flattened fifth. Otherwise, the flattened fifth can be played *below* the seventh and third, without interrupting the voice leading in the top line.

In the following example, the **flattened fifth** above the minor seventh chord is repeated as the **flattened ninth** above the dominant seventh chord, and then descends chromatically to form the **fifth** above the minor seventh chord:

Figure 8-14

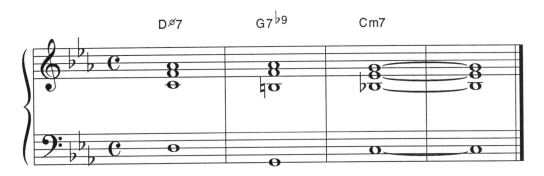

In the following example, two alternative voicings are shown for the half-diminished seventh chord: one with the **ninth**, the other with the **flattened fifth**. In each case, the top line descends by step or half step to form the **flattened thirteenth** above the dominant seventh chord, and then descends chromatically to form the **ninth** above the minor seventh chord:

Figure 8-15

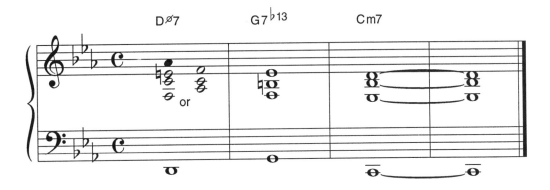

PLAYING CHORD PROGRESSIONS IN FOUR PARTS

Being able to play both major and minor II-V-I cadences fluently in all keys will provide the key to playing entire chord progression in four parts. To some extent the introduction of a fourth line can be seen as further reharmonization, since it is an optional elaboration of the basic chord symbols.   Since the language of jazz has evolved gradually through a process **improvisation** and **elaboration**, we are constantly faced with numerous harmonic choices. With this in mind, the most that any book can do is to provide clear and concise musical examples that suggest how coherent musical choices can be made.

The following example shows a typical eight-bar chord progression as it might be played in four parts. You can hear how the new fourth line is heard as a **counter-melody**:

Figure 8-16

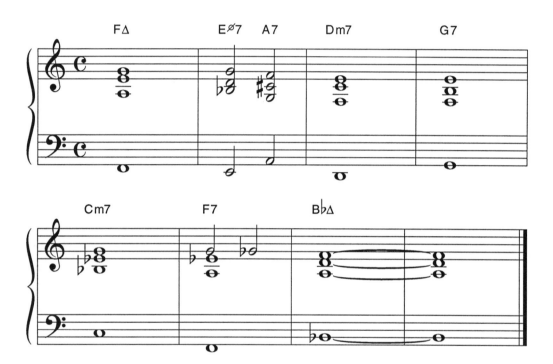

Please note the following:

• We learned that when playing three-part chordal accompaniments, the voicings chosen should lie just below the melodic line, this also proved crucial when the melody and chords were played together in *Chapter Six*. Similarly, four-part chords should generally lie just below the melodic line, though when **accompanying** a singer or instrumentalist, the top line of the chords can coincide with, or be played above, the melodic line without sounding dissonant.

• As with three-part harmony, **voicing shifts** will be needed to keep the chords in the same area of the keyboard. In **Figure 8-16** a voicing shift occurs between bars 4 and 5.

• Always **listen** carefully to the chords you are playing, it will usually be obvious which extension interval sounds best.

INTERPRETING EXTENSIONS

When reading chord symbols, extension intervals will often be symbolized.

For example: **G7♭9**

This chord symbol clearly suggests a G7 chord with a flattened ninth.

Q. But how should it be interpreted within the context of a chord progression?

A. If the register of the voicings we are playing lead us to a position where the *ninths* are the available extension intervals *above* the G7 chord base (as shown in **Figure 8-2**), clearly the flattened ninth should be played in preference to the natural or sharpened ninth. But if the register of the voicings we are playing lead us to the alternative voicing of G7, where the sharpened eleventh, fifth, flattened or natural thirteenth are the available extension intervals above the G7 chord base (as shown in **Figure 8-3**), one from this group should be chosen.

In other words, the flattened ninth symbol should be observed or ignored *depending on which voicing is played*, thereby maintaining a smooth fourth line above the chord base. Remember that at this stage, we are not inserting extensions intervals within or below the chord base.

The chord in the second bar of "Stella by Starlight" is normally symbolized with a flattened ninth, to coincide with the flattened ninth in the melody. This is clearly to alert the accompanist to the melodic line, implying that a natural ninth would create a dissonance. In the following example, a **flattened ninth** is chosen as the fourth part of the chord:

Figure 8-17

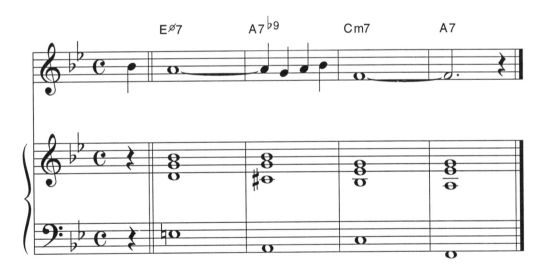

If we were playing alternative voicings, the flattened ninth symbol could be ignored in favour of an extension interval chosen from the second group (**Figure 8-3**). In the following example, a **flattened thirteenth** is played above the dominant seventh chord, thereby maintaining a smooth harmonic line below the melody:

Figure 8-18

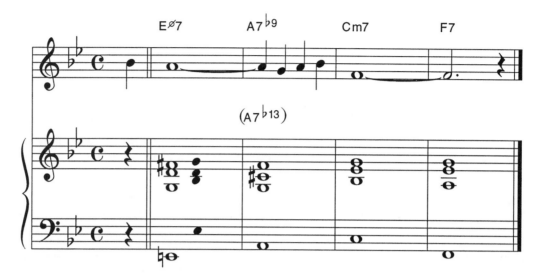

Please note the following:

• Extension intervals are generally symbolized for one of two reasons: firstly, to indicate an underlying harmonic progression, for example: a half-diminished seventh chord implies the II of a minor II-V-I cadence; or secondly, to indicate a potential dissonance that may arise between the melody and the accompaniment. This is particularly common with dominant seventh chords, where the accompanist can choose from several intervals, some of which will be dissonant to the melodic line.

• Extension symbols say as much about which intervals should *not* be played as about which should be played. For example: a dominant seventh chord with a thirteenth symbol suggests that any extension interval can be played with the exception of the flattened thirteenth.

• In more advanced chord charts, extension intervals will also be used to indicate very specific voicings. As the harmony becomes more complex, composers often prefer to write out the chords in full, rather than leave it to imprecise symbols.

• Dominant seventh chords with natural ninths and thirteenths as extension intervals can also be abbreviated:

$$G7^{13} \qquad \textit{can also be symbolized} \qquad G13$$

$$G7^{9} \qquad \textit{can also be symbolized} \qquad G9$$

• Resist the temptation to insert extension intervals within or below the chord base until the voice-leading principles shown here have been fully absorbed. In *Chapter Ten*, a fifth part will be introduced that will place extension intervals above, within and below the chord base.

• Chord symbols should never be interpreted too literally, rather they are an indication of the intended harmonic accompaniment. Furthermore, they are often inaccurate or imprecise. Attention must always be paid to the overall shape of the harmonic line, particularly when accompanying singers, when the counter melody created by the fourth part provides crucial support to the main theme.

RESOLVING THE NINTH

We have already seen how the ninth can be replaced by the less strident flattened fifth below the seventh and third in half-diminished seventh chords (**Figure 8-8**). The strident quality of the ninth can also be "defused" by a resolution to the octave (tonic), a device that can also be interpreted as a second to tonic **suspension** (2-1). This is particularly effective with minor seventh chords. With major seventh chords, it can also be combined with a resolution of the major seventh to the sixth.

In the following example, the **ninth** (second) resolves to the **octave** (tonic), without altering the harmonic function of the chord:

Figure 8-19

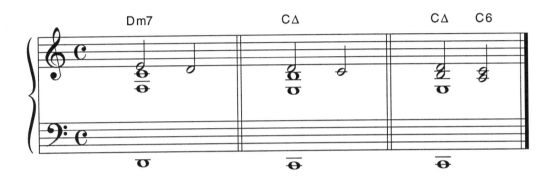

THE MINOR ELEVENTH CHORD

An alternative to playing the fifth above the minor seventh chord is to play the **eleventh** (fourth). Referred to as a **minor eleventh** chord, it is often appears where the eleventh is the melody note. It also makes it possible to play the dominant note (G) as the fourth part for all three chords in the II-V-I cadence:

Figure 8-20

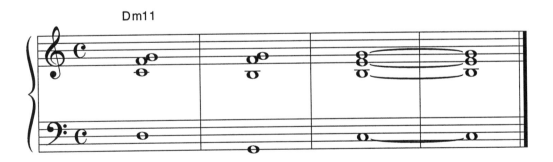

EXTENSIONS FOR SECONDARY JAZZ CHORDS

In *Chapter Two*, five **secondary** jazz chords were introduced:

1) the **augmented major seventh**
2) the **augmented seventh**
3) the **minor-major seventh**
4) the **major sixth**
5) the **minor sixth**

When playing chord progressions in three-parts, these chords were not fully defined due to the omission of the fifth - by reintroducing the fifth as a fourth part, their full harmonic composition will be revealed. In each case two voicings are shown: the first introduces the fifth to fully define the chord (perfect, augmented or diminished); the second introduces an alternative fourth part which can be played wherever the chord symbol appears, and priority needs to be given to maintaining good voice-leading:

Figure 8-21

1) The **augmented major seventh** chord, **CΔaug, C+Δ**:

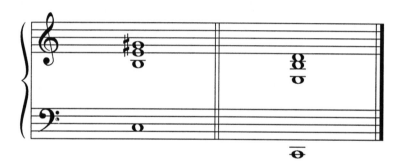

2) The **augmented dominant seventh** chord, **C7aug, C+7, C7♭13**:

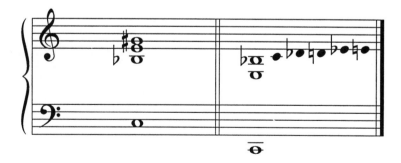

3) The **minor-major seventh** chord, Cm△:

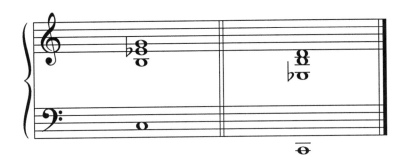

4) The **major sixth** chord, **C6**:

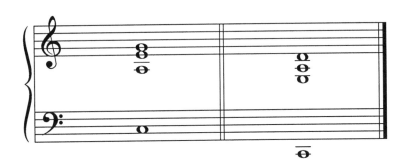

5) The **minor sixth** chord, **Cm6**:

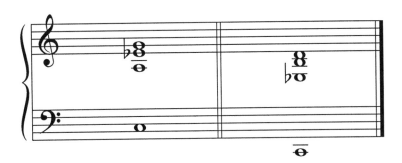

REHARMONIZATION AND THE FOURTH PART

Finally, the reharmonizations shown in the previous chapter can be introduced into four-part chord progressions. Shown here are some reharmonizations of the II-V-I cadences, notice that the fourth part often changes for the reharmonised chord.

Introducing the suspended fourth in four parts:

In the first example, a suspension is introduced with the ninth as a fourth part. The ninth then descends chromatically together with the resolution of the fourth to the third:

Figure 8-22

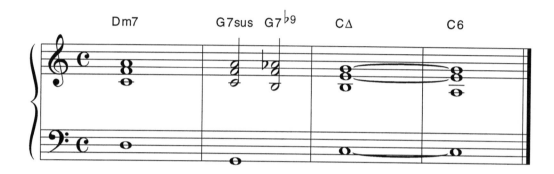

In the alternative voicing, the thirteenth provides a fourth part for the suspended chord, descending chromatically together with the resolution of the fourth to the third:

Figure 8-23

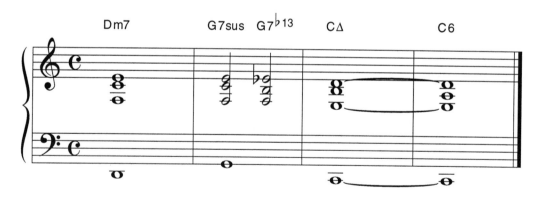

Introducing the minor-major to minor seventh in four parts:

In the following example, the fifth is introduced above the minor-major to minor seventh resolution, becoming the ninth of the dominant seventh chord. Notice that in this example, only the moving parts are played:

Figure 8-24

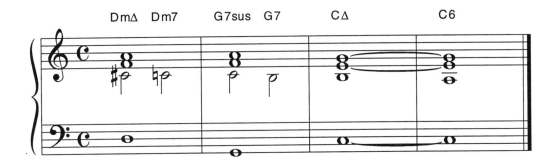

In the following example, the ninth is introduced above the minor-major to minor seventh resolution, becoming the thirteenth of the dominant seventh chord. Again, only the moving parts are played:

Figure 8-25

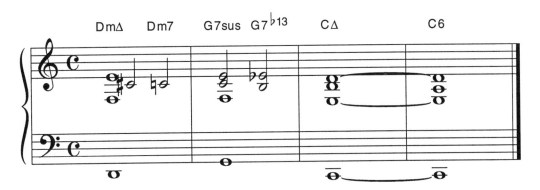

Introducing the major seventh - dominant seventh in four parts:

In the following example, the ninth descends chromatically to the flattened-ninth together with the major seventh to dominant seventh resolution:

Figure 8-26

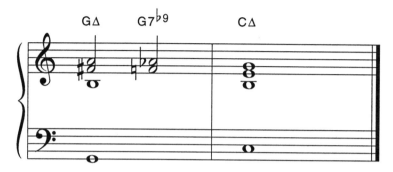

In the following example, the thirteenth descends chromatically to the flattened-thirteenth together with the major seventh to dominant seventh resolution:

Figure 8-27

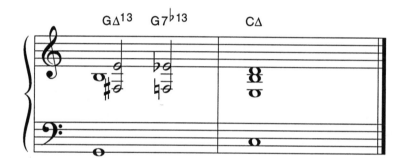

Introducing the chromatic shift in four parts:

In the following example, the entire dominant seventh chord + flattened fifth is approached chromatically from *above:*

Figure 8-28

downwards:

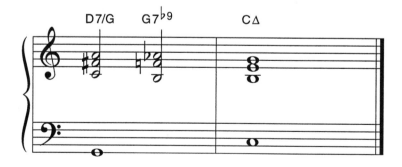

or alternatively:

Figure 8-29

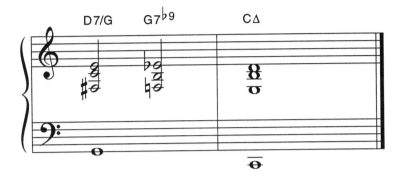

In the following example, the entire dominant seventh chord + flattened fifth is approached chromatically from *below:*

Figure 8-30

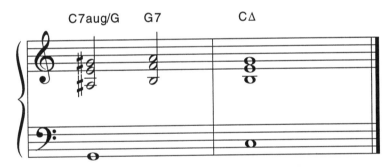

or alternatively,

Figure 8-31

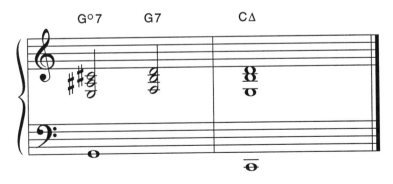

Introducing tritone substitution in four parts:

Finally, tritone substitution can be introduced into a four-part II-V-I cadence:

Figure 8-32

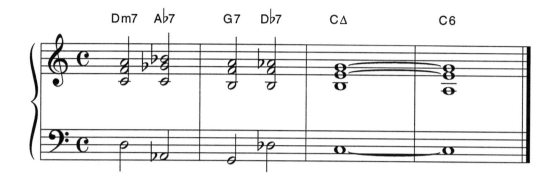

or alternatively,

Figure 8-33

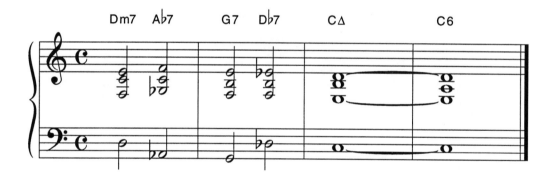

Exercises:

i) Practice playing and transposing **Figures 8-22** to **8-33**.

ii) Play through the chord progression of a standard song, introducing a fourth part above the three-part chords.

iii) Play through the same chord progression introducing some reharmonization as shown at the end of this chapter.

MUSICAL EXAMPLE

Shown below is a typical chord progression that includes most of what we has been introduced in this chapter. A **counter-melody** is introduced above the chord base, while reharmonization is introduced to create additional harmonic interest. The chords are played on each beat of the bar to create a steady pulse.

Figure 8-34

CHAPTER NINE

PLAYING THE MELODY II

In this chapter, we shall learn how to play the melody and **four-part** chords together. The approach will be the same as for three-part chords, as shown in *Chapter Six*, but with an additional fourth line or **counter melody** inserted *between* the melody and chords. Again, it will be crucial to observe the voice-leading principles learned in previous chapters.

PLAYING THE MELODY WITH FOUR-PART CHORDS

In *Chapter Five*, the melody and chords were played together for the first time. Furthermore, two different approaches were used: a shorthand approach, where the voicings chosen lay immediately below the melodic line; and a longhand approach, where the voicings chosen adhered more closely to voice-leading principles. We shall use the **longhand** approach to make the best possible arrangement of the **melody** and **four-part** chords.

In the following example, the first eight bars of "Stella by Starlight" are played using the longhand approach. It is significant that the third and seventh are spread across both hands and played *around* or *below* middle C, leaving ample space for a fourth part to be inserted *between* the chords and the melodic line:

Figure 9-1

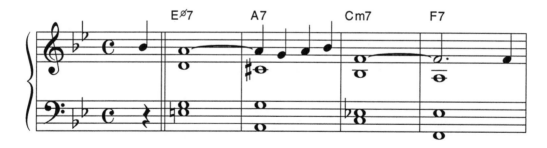

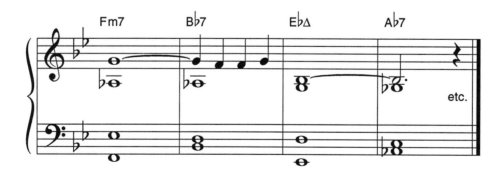

In *Chapter Eight*, we learned how to play chordal accompaniments using four-part chords. The accompaniment for the first eight bars of "Stella by Starlight" might be as follows:

Figure 9-2

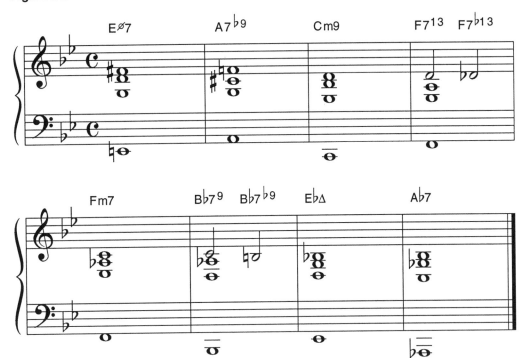

Notice that the top line of the above chords produces a strong **counter-melody**:

Figure 9-3

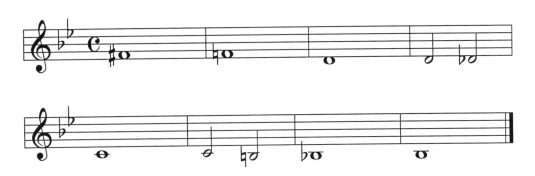

The fourth part can be introduced into the arrangement of the song by spreading the chords across both hands as and when necessary. Notice that the melody and fourth part **merge** in the final two bars:

Figure 9-4

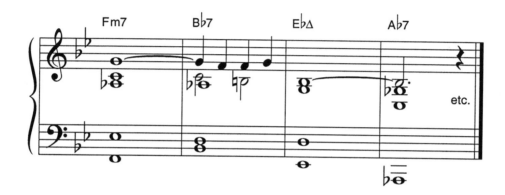

MUSICAL EXAMPLES

Shown here are some song extracts that include four-part accompaniment chords.

In the first example, the opening bars "My Ideal" are shown. A **counter-melody** is played between the top line of the chords and the melody:

Figure 9-5

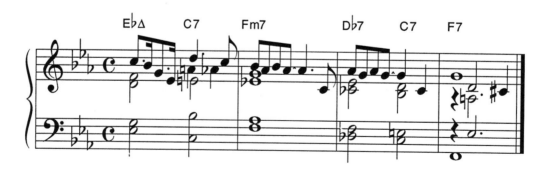

The opening of Axel Stordhal, Paul Weston and Sammy Cahn's "Day by Day" builds up to a II-V-I cadence in G major, followed by a passage through the cycle of fifths. The melodic leaps in the first six bars is contained by alternating between spreading the chords across both hands (bars 1, 3 and 5) and playing the entire chord in the right-hand (bars 2 and 4). **Rhythmic displacement** is introduced to accompany the held notes in the last two bars:

Figure 9-6

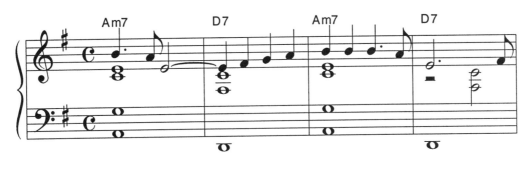

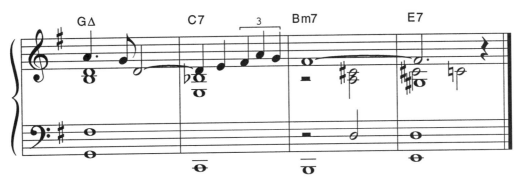

In the first and third bar of "My Old Flame", the break in the right-hand chord needed play the melody can be masked by using the sustain pedal. In the second bar, the flattened fifth interval is played below the seventh and third for a "mellow" voicing that leads smoothly to the next chord. There is also a **voicing shift** *upwards* between the second and third bar in tandem with the melody:

Figure 9-7

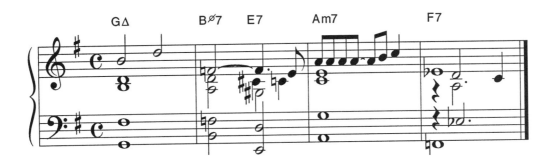

The pick-up to "If I Should Lose You" sounds especially dramatic with the introduction of a sharpened ninth between the melody and the chord base. In the penultimate bar, the third and seventh are both taken into the left-hand to contain the octave leap in the melody:

Figure 9-8

A counter-melody can be introduced into the opening phrase of "Girl Talk." In the last two bars, **lower voicings** are played to provide space four the fourth part between the chords and the melody:

Figure 9-9

The first eight bars of Ralph Rainer and Leo Robin's "Easy Living" include substantial leaps up and down the chord tones. In such cases, the **sustain pedal** can be used to mask any unavoidable breaks in the harmonic line:

Figure 9-10

INTRODUCING REHARMONIZATION

Shown below are some song extracts that have been arranged to demonstrate how the melody, four-part chords and reharmonization can be played simultaneously. After analysing each example, the knowledge acquired should be immediately transferred to other songs in a similar style.

The opening phrase of Hoagy Carmichael and Ned Washington's "The Nearness of You" can be effectively reharmonized by introducing an **pedal note** (F) throughout the first four bars. Notice that in bar 3, the tonic has been introduced in the left-hand to give the second inversion chord more weight. In bar 4, the diminished-seventh chord is **revoiced** using the same notes on the second beat and moves in tandem with the melody:

Figure 9-11

The dominant seventh chord in bars 2 and 4 of "Never Let Me Go" can include a **suspension**, as well as a ninth to flattened ninth **chromatic descent** in the fourth part:

Figure 9-12

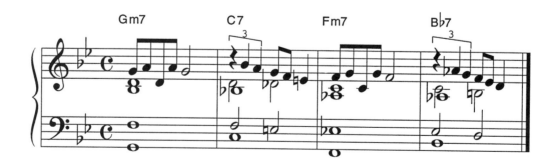

In the first four bars of "It's Easy to Remember", a counter-melody can be introduced between the chords and the melody. Notice that a 2-1 **suspension** is played in the first bar, and that exceptionally the fourth part is played *between* the seventh and third in bars 2 and 3:

Figure 9-13

The second bar of "My Old Flame" sounds extremely dissonant yet resolves in a logical way when reharmonized. Notice also that harmonic motion is introduced in the third bar by moving from a **minor seventh** to a **minor-major seventh** chord, then back to a minor seventh chord on the last beat of the bar:

Figure 9-14

In the last example, a **steady pulse** is introduced into the bridge section of "Easy Living." Notice a voicing shift occurs on bars 2 and 4 in tandem with the melody:

Figure 9-15

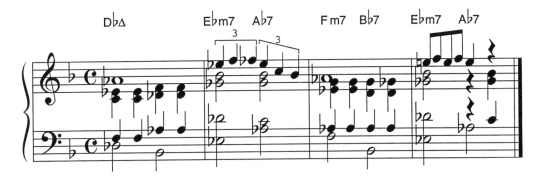

THE MINOR ELEVENTH CHORD IN FOUR PARTS

The following example provides an alternative to the minor seventh voicing where the ninth is played as a fourth part. The minor eleventh interval can be played as a fourth *above* the tonic and *below* the seventh and third, making a chord of **compound fourths**. This is often referred to as **quartal harmony** and will be discussed more fully later in the book, it is best introduced when the melody note is either the minor third or fifth of the minor seventh chord:

Figure 9-16

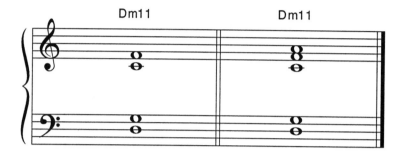

In bar 25 of "Tangerine," the melody begins on the fifth of Gm7 and descends immediately to the third, the phrase is then repeated down a fourth in bar 27. In each case, the melody is harmonized by the minor eleventh voicing shown in **Figure 9-16**:

Figure 9-17

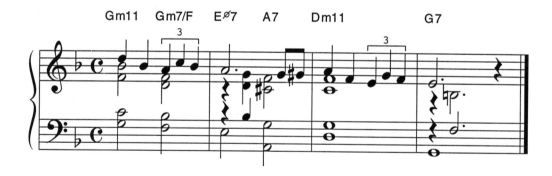

ALTERNATIVE VOICINGS FOR THE SUSPENSION

A useful voicing for the suspension chord can be created by inserting the ninth *between* the seventh and fourth interval, and for it to descend chromatically to the flattened ninth for the resolution:

Figure 9-18

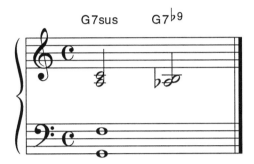

The opening passage of Richard Rodgers and Oscar Hammerstein II's "Hello Young Lovers," features alternation between the tonic and dominant seventh chord of C major. The dominant can also be played as a suspension, furthermore, the voicing shown in **Figure 9-18** is played in bar 4 where the melody dips down to an E. The flattened-ninth is also played *between* the third and seventh in bar 6, thereby creating a smooth harmonic line:

Figure 9-19

The opening phrase of Burt Bacharach and Hal David's "Alfie" features a suspension in the second bar. The most effective way to harmonize the melodic leap in the this bar is to insert a ninth between the seventh and third. Notice also that a sixth chord is played in preference to the major seventh chord in the first bar: this is normally a very acceptable reharmonization, particularly where the melody begins on the fifth and a compound fourth chord can be played:

Figure 9-20

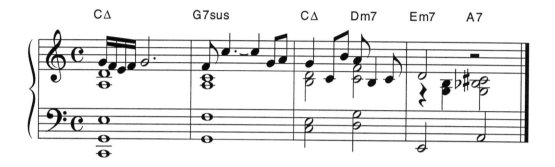

In the last example, the bridge passage of Richard Rodgers and Oscar Hammerstein II's "It Might As Well Be Spring" is shown. A minor eleventh chord is played in bar 2 and becomes a suspension in bar 3. Notice also that in bar 6, the F# in the bass is held over to the B7 chord, creating a **second inversion** chord. In the final bar, the suspension is "decorated" by passing via the second before resolving to the third:

Figure 9-21

Please note the following:

• When the melody and chords are played together, care must be taken to avoid playing undesirable dissonances. Dissonances that might go unnoticed when accompanying an instrumentalist or singer will be more pronounced when played on the piano.

• In the previous musical examples, held notes are sometimes written though they cannot be held for their full value, since other notes need to be played. In such circumstances, the **sustain pedal** can be used to mask any breaks in the melodic or harmonic line.

• Each example has been carefully written to demonstrate the skill needed to play jazz piano. It makes sense to study each extract in detail, to ensure that each harmonic device is fully understood and integrated into your own style before moving onto more complex harmony.

PRACTICING MUSICAL PATTERNS

We are now at a point where much of the information acquired needs to be practiced for greater accuracy and technical fluency. With this in mind, it is a good moment to pause in the learning process and put some effort into "automating" what we have learned. We can do this by analysing some of the musical phrases that constantly reappear and simply turn them into **musical patterns**. Outlined below is a procedure for practicing musical patterns:

Procedure:

1) Play through a standard song and pause on any interesting musical phrase. Analyse it to fully understand its **melodic** and **harmonic structure**.

2) If necessary **simplify** the melody so that it becomes suitable for transposition.

3) Experiment with various **reharmonizations** and **rhythmic displacements**.

4) Play each pattern *ascending* the **chromatic** scale.

5) Play each pattern *descending* the **chromatic** scale.

6) Play each pattern moving through the **cycle of fifths**.

For example, we might select the following phrase based on the II-V of a II-V-I cadence:

Figure 9-22

Having played this phrase a few times and experimented with various rhythmic displacements and reharmonizations, the following version can serve as our musical pattern:

Figure 9-23

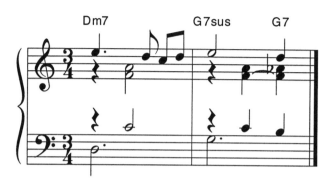

Analysis:

The extract is in 3/4 time and is based on the II-V of a II-V-I cadence in C. The melody begins on the ninth of Dm7 and is accompanied by its tonic in the bass, the chord itself includes the fifth as a fourth part and is delayed to the second beat of the bar. The second bar begins on the same melody note as the first bar (E) and is accompanied by its tonic in the bass, the chord is again delayed to the second beat of the bar. A suspension precedes the G7 chord and includes the ninth as a fourth part, it then descends to a flattened ninth together with the resolution to the dominant seventh chord on the last beat of the bar. The melody and chords are spread evenly across both hands throughout the example.

Transposing Musical Patterns:

The phrase can now be transposed into all twelve keys as follows:

Firstly, **ascending** the chromatic scale:

Figure 9-24

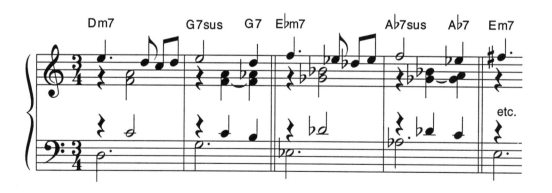

Secondly, **descending** the chromatic scale:

Figure 9-25

Thirdly, moving through the **cycle of fifths**:

Figure 9-26

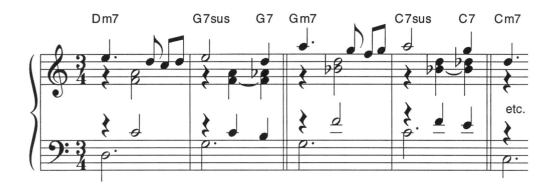

Please note the following:

• This is a good time to begin compiling your own **glossary of musical patterns**, this should be a personal book of musical phrases that can be referred to and practiced in all keys.

• Transposition is the best way of **learning** the keyboard. To be able to play anything from a simple melody to an entire sequence of chords in any key without hesitation is an essential skill for a jazz pianist.

• The task of transposition is made much easier by the fact that most standard songs refer to the same underlying harmonic vocabulary, since most variation is found in the melody. Having become efficient at playing the underlying harmonic structures, slight variations to the melodic line can be made with little difficulty.

PROCEDURE

Having acquired a facility to play chordal accompaniments in four parts, with and without the melody, and having experimented with various forms of reharmonization and transposition, the following **ten-stage procedure** can now be adopted when learning a new song:

a) Play the **melody**.

b) Play the melody together with the **bass notes** (as indicated by the symbols).

c) Play through the chord progression in **three-parts**, observing the voice-leading principles shown in *Chapter Three*.

d) Finding firstly the melody note, secondly the bass note, and thirdly the right-hand voicing that is within your reach below the melody line, play through the song adopting the **shorthand** approach.

e) Finding firstly the melody note, secondly the bass note, and thirdly the voicing that adheres to voice-leading principles, play through the song adopting the **longhand** approach.

 f) Play through the chord progression introducing **reharmonizations** where appropriate, as shown in *Chapter Seven*.

g) Play through the chord progression in four-parts, creating a smooth **counter-melody** in the top part, as shown in *Chapter Eight*, introducing reharmonizations where appropriate.

h) Finding firstly the melody note, secondly the bass note, and thirdly the **four-part** voicing that adheres to voice-leading principles, play through the song adopting the **longhand** approach.

i) Introduce some **reharmonization** where appropriate.

j) Introduce some **rhythmic displacement** referring to the accompaniment models shown in *Chapter Five*, to create a more animated and musical arrangement of the song.

k) Write down any song extracts you find appealing in your personal glossary of **musical patterns**.

• For a list of suitable songs, refer to the **Song To Select** shown at the end of *Chapter Four*.

CHAPTER TEN

FIVE-PART HARMONY

In *Chapter Eight*, a fourth part was introduced above the three-part chord base. In this chapter we shall continue this building process by introducing a **fifth part**. As we shall see, the voice-leading principles learned in previous chapters will continue to be of crucial importance.

FIVE-PART CHORDS IN OPEN-POSITION

In *Chapter Eight*, we learned that a four-part jazz chord can be created by introducing any one of ten extension intervals above the dominant seventh chord base, the two remaining intervals that could not be used because they sounded too dissonant, were the fourth and major third. The result was two groups of extension intervals, shown previously as group a) and b) (**Figures 8-2** and **8-3**).

Q. What would happen if an extension interval from each group be played simultaneously above the chord base?

Figure 10-1

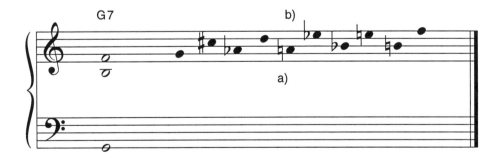

or alternatively,

Figure 10-2

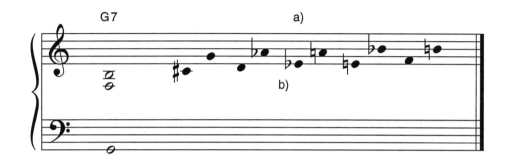

A. By playing any two of the above extension intervals simultaneously, one from each group, a rich variety of chordal possibilities are created, each with its own particular **resonance**:

Figure 10-3

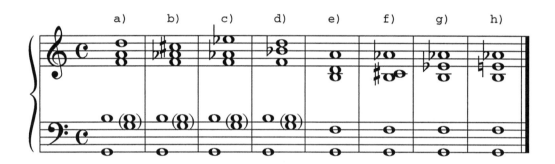

Key:

a) G7^9 (or G9)

b) G7$^{\flat 9/\sharp 11}$

c) G7$^{\flat 9/\flat 13}$

d) G7$^{\sharp 9}$

e) G7^9 (or G9)

f) G7$^{\flat 9/\sharp 11}$

g) G7$^{\flat 9/\flat 13}$

h) G7$^{\flat 9/13}$

Please note the following:

• All the chords shown in **Figure 10-3** have been created by randomly selecting one interval from each group, and playing them simultaneously above the dominant seventh chord base. Since there are five extension intervals in each group, five x five = twenty-five: there are **twenty-five** alternative voicings for the dominant seventh when played in five parts.

• Extension intervals should be symbolized with the smallest interval first and the largest interval last, irrespective of the order in which they are played:

$$\text{G7}^{\flat9/\sharp11}$$

• The brackets may be added to differentiate between the chord and the extension intervals:

$$\text{G7}^{(\flat9/\sharp11)}$$

• Alternatively, they can be shown the same size and in a straight line:

$$\text{G7}(\flat9/\sharp11)$$

• Finally, they can also be shown stacked on top of each other:

$$\text{G7}^{(\sharp11)}_{(\flat9)}$$

SLASH CHORDS

Chord b) in **Figure 10-3** (G7$^{\flat9/\sharp11}$) could also have been symbolized as a **slash chord**. These are created by placing one chord structure (usually a triad) above an unrelated chord base. We shall learn about polychords and upper-structure triads in the next chapter, but for now we can see that the chord shown in **Figure 10-3** could have been described as a D♭ major triad played over a G7 chord base:

Figure 10-4

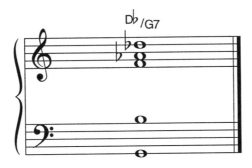

FIVE-PART MINOR SEVENTH CHORDS

Though it is possible to play a variety of extension intervals above a dominant seventh chord, the same freedom cannot be extended to **minor seventh** chords, as several extensions will sound extremely dissonant. In order to begin the process of building five-part jazz chords, we must introduce the following restriction:

Restriction:

The **fifth** and **ninth** are the only extension intervals that can be played simultaneously above **minor seventh** chords:

Figure 10-5

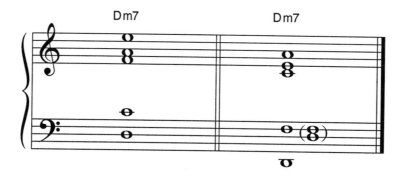

FIVE-PART MAJOR SEVENTH CHORDS

The same restriction must be applied to **major seventh** chords:

Restriction:

The **fifth** and **ninth** are the only extension intervals that can be played simultaneously above **major seventh** chords:

Figure 10-6

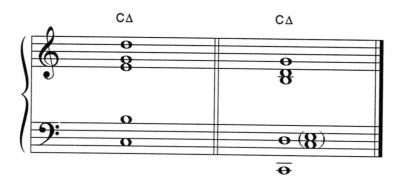

Please note the following:

• Chords shown so far are In **open-position** with all extension intervals played *above* the three-part chord base.

• **Dominant seventh** chords combine an extension interval from group a) and b) to create twenty-five possible combinations for each voicing, as shown in **Figures 10-1** and **10-2**.

• **Minor** and **major seventh** chords combine the fifth and the ninth to create two possible combinations for each voicing, as shown in **Figure 10-5** and **10-6**. It is helpful to begin by adopting the restrictions shown, however alternative voicings will be introduced later in the chapter.

• Many of the chordal combinations shown here have already been heard, where the melody note has provided the fifth part. But as we shall see, these new five-part chords can be played together with the an additional melody note, resulting in a six-part chordal structure.

• These open-position voicings are extremely effective on the piano and are particularly useful when accompanying a singer or instrumentalist.

VARIATIONS

After having practiced the "restricted" five-part voicings for minor and major seventh chords, some variations can be introduced. They can all be freely introduced into our arrangements of standard songs:

1) Half-diminished seventh chords

In the following example, the fifth is played as a diminished fifth:

Figure 10-7

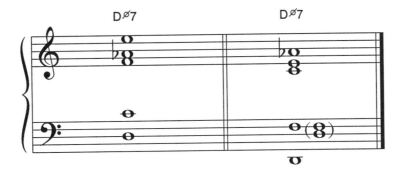

---

2) Minor eleventh chords

In the following example, the fifth is replaced by the eleventh for minor seventh chords:

Figure 10-8

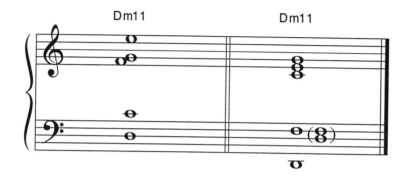

3) Sharpened fourth chords

In the following example, the fifth is replaced by a sharpened fourth for major seventh chords:

Figure 10-9

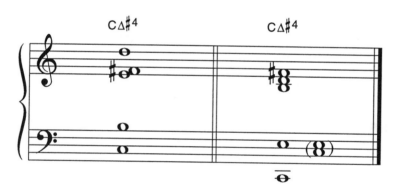

4) Octave or third replacing the ninth in minor seventh chords

Finally, the octave or third can replace the ninth in both minor and major seventh chords to create a less "strident" sounding chord:

Figure 10-10

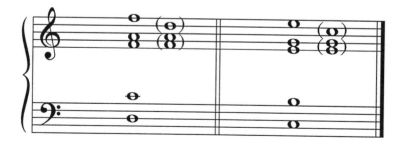

THE II-V-I CADENCE IN FIVE PARTS

The voice-leading principles adhered to in previous chapters continue to be crucial when playing five-part chord progressions. In the following examples, the fourth and fifth parts are shown to be fixed for chords II (minor seventh) and I (major seventh) of the II-V-I cadence, whereas there are twenty-five ways of playing chord V (dominant seventh):

Figure 10-11

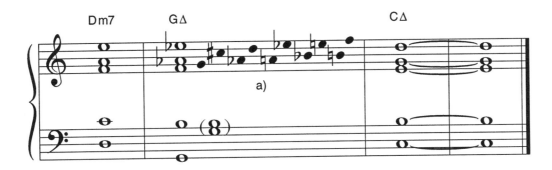

or alternatively:

Figure 10-12

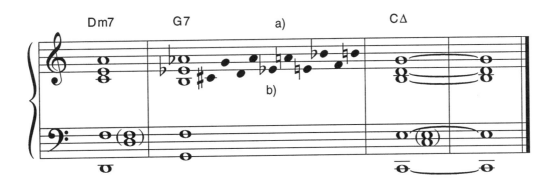

The extension intervals can also change *during* the dominant seventh chord:

Figure 10-13

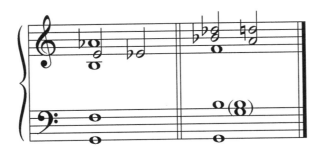

Exercises:

i) Practice playing the II-V-I cadences shown in **Figures 10-12** and **10-13** in all keys.

ii) Introduce some of the variations shown previously (**Figures 10-7** to **10-11**).

MUSICAL EXAMPLES

In the following example, an accompaniment to "The Nearness of You" consists of five-part open-position chords. Notice that a steady pulse is introduced from the beginning to set the mood of a ballad, reharmonization is introduced throughout and some notes are held in the upper parts during last four bars:

Figure 10-14

In "You Brought a New Kind Of Love To Me" a more rhythmic and jazzy accompaniment is shown. Notice that chords are repeated and syncopated and that the interplay between the chords and the bass notes is particularly effective:

Figure 10-15

PLAYING THE MELODY WITH FIVE-PART CHORDS

There are occasions when the melodic line of a song moves into a high register, in such cases it is sometimes desirable to introduce a fifth part into the accompanying chords. This will result in a total of **six** parts including the melody.

The bridge section of "Stella by Starlight" is in a high register and provides an ideal occasion for five-part accompaniment chords. Notice that the chords are rhythmically displaced to add some harmonic motion during held melody notes.

Figure 10-16

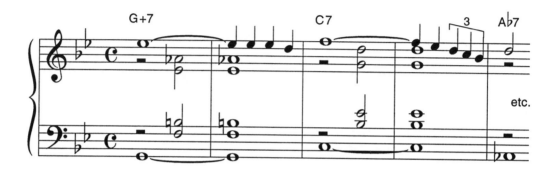

or alternatively with reharmonization:

Figure 10-17

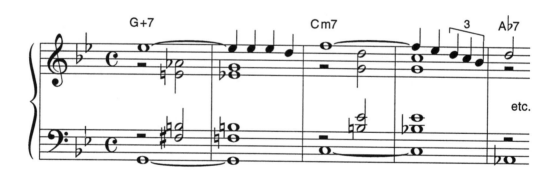

Please note the following:
• The large stretches needed to play five or six-part chords can often be facilitated by either spreading the chords across two hands, rhythmically displacing the chords or the bass notes, or using the sustain pedal to mask any undesirable breaks in the harmonic line.

• For a clear a concise accompaniment style, ensure that the third, seventh and extension interval(s) are all played simultaneously, and that only the chord as a whole or the bass note is rhythmically displaced.

• When accompanying an instrumentalist or singer, the register of the upper parts can rise above the register of the melody provided they do not create dissonance. Notice that the voicings chosen in the previous examples carefully avoid notes that would be dissonant with the melody.

• Five-part secondary jazz chords follow the same procedure as five-part primary jazz chords.

FIVE-PART CHORDS IN CLOSED-POSITION

Until now, extension intervals have been shown above the three-part chord base, this made good sense not only because it created very usable and effective chords, but also because it engendered an awareness of voice leading and the harmonic line when playing chord progressions. However, there is no reason why extension intervals cannot now be played *within* or *below* the chord base, and follow the same voice-leading principles. As we shall see, the chords produced are of much greater density and harmonic richness.

In the following examples, the fifth part of each chord of the II-V-I cadence shown previously has been transposed down by an octave to *within* the chord base. We shall refer to these new chords as five-part **closed-position** voicings. They have a particularly "crunchy" sound and are frequently taught as standard left-hand accompaniment voicings to be played when soloing in the right-hand while accompanied by a bass player:

The Minor Seventh Chord:

Figure 10-18

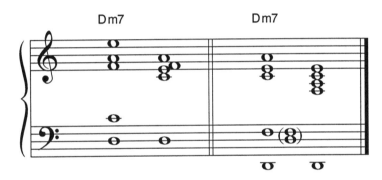

The Dominant Seventh Chord:

Figure 10-19

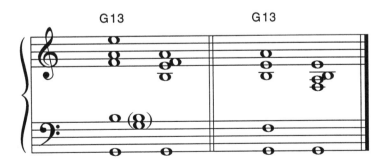

or alternatively:

Figure 10-20

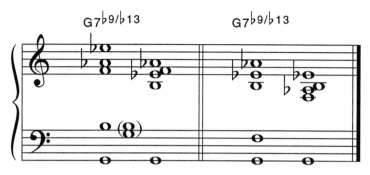

The Major Seventh Chord:

Figure 10-21

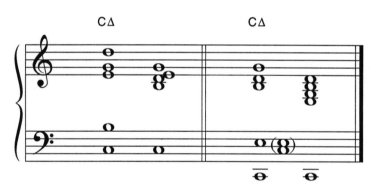

CLOSED-POSITION CHORDS AND THE II-V-I CADENCE

The chords can also be shown as part of a II-V-I cadence:

Figure 10-22

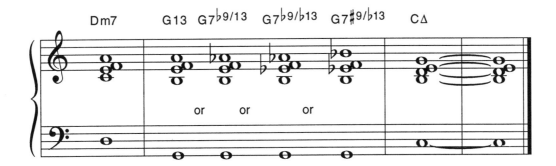

or alternatively:

Figure 10-23

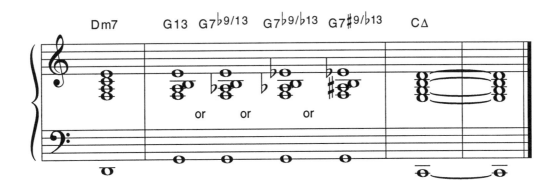

Exercise:

Practice transposing the II-V-I cadences shown in **Figures 10-22** and **10-23** into all keys.

VARIATIONS

There are several variations that can be introduced for both the minor seventh and major seventh chords when playing five-part closed-position voicings.

THE MINOR ELEVENTH CHORD

The minor eleventh chord shown in **Figure 10-8** can be played as a closed-position voicing:

Figure 10-24

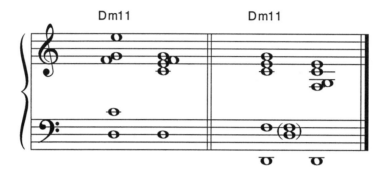

THE MAJOR SEVENTH/SIXTH CHORD

A new voicing can be created that includes both the major seventh and major sixth interval, without the fifth. It would be symbolized as C△6:

Figure 10-25

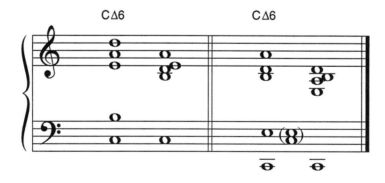

REHARMONIZATION AND FIVE-PART CLOSED-POSITION CHORDS

Reharmonization can also be applied to five-part closed-position chords. The fourth and fifth parts can also *change* during the reharmonized chord as the following examples demonstrate:

Figure 10-26

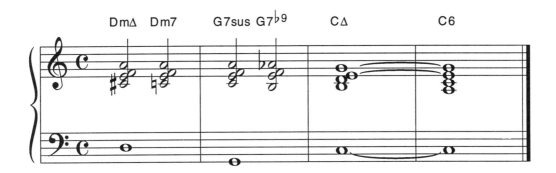

or alternatively:

Figure 10-27

INVERTING CLOSED-POSITION CHORDS

The chord shapes we are now playing closely resemble the closed-position jazz chords shown in *Chapter Two*, a four-note voicing contained within an octave. This means that they can also be **inverted**.

In the following examples, the closed-position voicings for the three chords in a II-V-I cadence are shown together with two new inversions:

The Minor Seventh Chord:

Figure 10-28

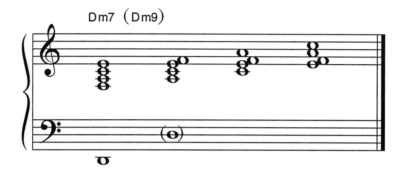

The Dominant Seventh Chord:

Figure 10-29

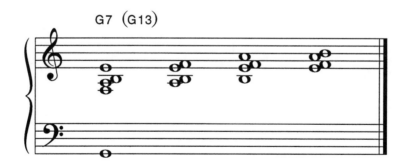

The Major Seventh Chord:

Figure 10-30

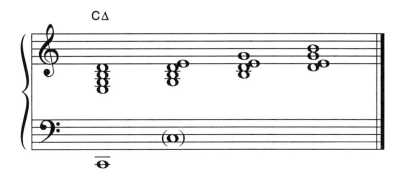

THE II-V-I CADENCE WITH FIVE-PART INVERTED CLOSED-POSITION CHORDS

These highly dense and percussive-sounding voicings can also be shown in a II-V-I cadence. Notice that they follow exactly the same voice-leading principles as the non-inverted voicings shown previously (**Figures 10-22** and **10-23**):

Figure 10-31

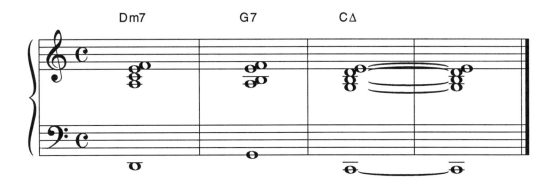

or alternatively:

Figure 10-32

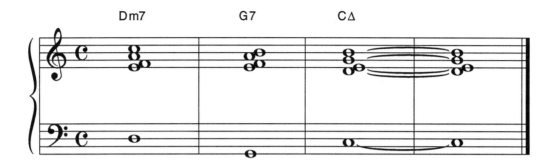

VOICE-LEADING WITH FIVE-PART INVERTED CLOSED-POSITION CHORDS

These new inversions can be used to make the voice leading in chord progressions even smoother. In the following example, the new inversions are introduced when moving between two unrelated II-V-I cadences, to create a smooth transition and harmonic line:

Figure 10-33

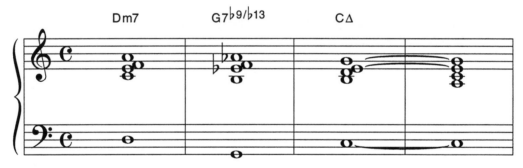

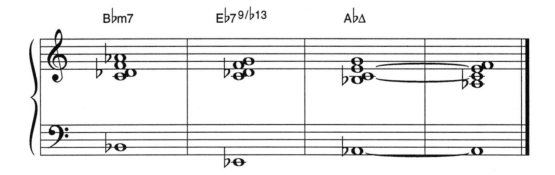

Please note the following:

• The melodic line will generally suggest which extension intervals should be chosen. Nevertheless, there is much scope for variation and reharmonization, particularly when accompanying solos. If you listen carefully to what you are playing and "trust you ears," it will become apparent which voicing sound best in each musical situation.

• Remember that the jazz pianist's aim is not harmonic density but rather the skilful handling of varying degrees of harmonic complexity.

• The closed-position voicings shown here can also be played as left-hand accompaniment voicings when playing with a bass player. The inverted chords shown in **Figures 10-28 to 10-33** sound particularly effective, providing a "punchy" and "crisp" accompaniment to solos.

• To be able to combine all the harmonic alternatives in a creative way will only come about with practice and greater familiarity with the jazz piano idiom. Listening extensively to the great jazz pianist is a prerequisite to playing good jazz piano. Pianists noted for there harmonic approach include the following:

Bill Evans

Keith Jarrett

Art Tatum

Herbie Hancock

Chick Corea

Oscar Peterson

Clare Fischer

Exercises:

i) Play the II-V- I cadence using five-part open and closed-position chords in all keys.

ii) Play through a standard chord progression using five-part closed-position voicings.

iii) Play through the same chord progression introducing some reharmonization.

iv) Play the five-part closed-position voicings in the left-hand to accompany a standard song.

v) Play through the same song introducing the inversions shown in **Figures 10-31** and **10-33**.

PLAYING THE MELODY WITH FIVE-PART CHORDS

We have already seen how open-position chords can be introduced when the melody is in a high register, **closed-position** chords can also be played to create a dense harmonic accompaniment to the melody. To make this new six-part structure playable, it will invariably be necessary to spread the chords across both hands and introduce rhythmic displacement.

In the first example, the opening phrase of "Stella by Starlight" is played with closed-position five-part voicings:

Figure 10-34

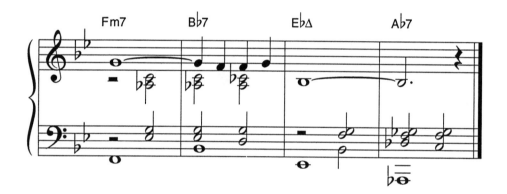

The first for bars of "Day by Day" alternates between the II and the V of a II-V-I cadence in G. The accompanying five-part voicings alternate between being spread across both hands and being played entirely by the right-hand:

Figure 10-35

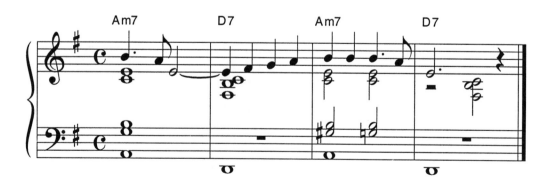

In the opening phrase of "It's Easy to Remember," a pedal B♭ provides a cushion for the subtly changing five-part harmony above:

Figure 10-36

Finally, the opening phrase of "If I Should Lose You" combines both open and closed-position voicings. The D7 chord in the third bar is a six-part chord, doubling the melody note *within* the chord. The final chord includes a sharpened fourth for dramatic effect - this is sometimes referred to as a **Lydian-tonic** chord:

Figure 10-37

PRACTICING MELODIC PATTERNS

The information in this chapter can best be internalised by devising **melodic patterns** that are suitable for transposition. Reharmonizations can also be added as and where appropriate.

In the following example, a melodic pattern based on a II-V-I cadence is shown, it refers to closed-position five-part harmony and is ideal for transposition:

Figure 10-38

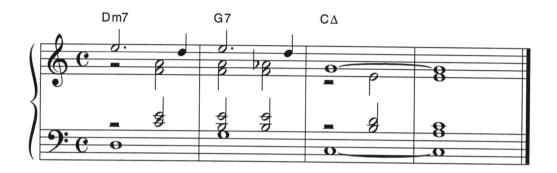

or alternatively:

Figure 10-39

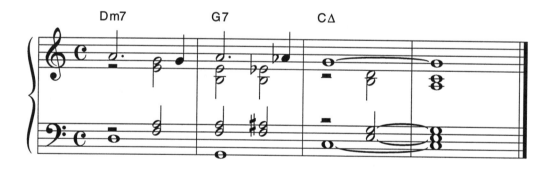

Exercise:

i) Practice the above two melodic patterns and transpose them into all twelve keys.

ii) Devise your own similar melodic patterns using open and closed-position five-part harmony, and transpose them into all twelve keys.

Conclusion:

• The three-part chords first introduced in *Chapter Three* has provided the harmonic basis for all the subsequent chapters. Inevitably, adding more parts and introducing reharmonization will create a richer and denser harmonic accompaniment, which may or may not be desirable depending on the musical context. Remember that complexity is not the jazz pianist's aim, but rather a resource that can be introduced as and when required. To be able to musically manipulate varying degrees of harmonic complexity and density is the ultimate goal.

An analogy could be made between building chords at the piano and adding spices when cooking: It is better to retain a clear concept of the dish you are trying to create and to gradually add the seasoning as a when required until the desired result is achieved.

• Remember that the chords should always **accompany** the melody and not dominate it. When playing standard songs a **volume balance** must be maintained between the melody and the chords. The primary function of the chords are to **accompany** the melody, and since the melody generally consists of a single line of notes, care must be taken to given the melody a little more weight and the chords a little less weight.

• Finally, the **sustain pedal** can always be used to mask any undesirable breaks in the harmonic line.

CHAPTER ELEVEN

POLYCHORDS & UPPER-STRUCTURE TRIADS

In this chapter, we shall see how **polytriads** and **upper-structure** triads can be used to build seven, eight and nine-part chords. Voice-leading will be continue to be crucial, particularly in the upper parts where the harmonic line is clearly heard.

POLYTRIADS

The triad is the basic unit of tonal harmony. The third defines a triad as being either major or minor, while the fifth can be either perfect, diminished or augmented resulting in four basic triads: **major**, **minor**, **diminished** and **augmented**, each playable in three positions or inversions: root position, first inversion and second inversion:

Figure 11-1

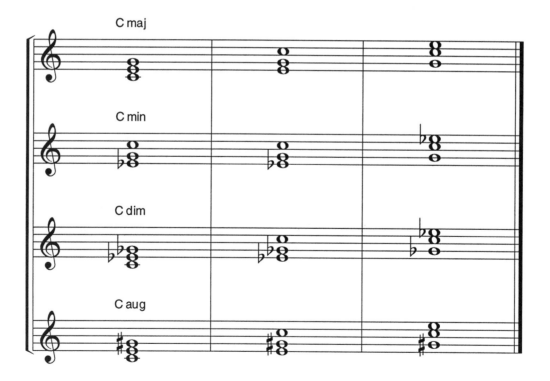

Triads can be stacked or super-imposed upon one another to produce diverse chordal shapes or **polytriads**:

Figure 11-2

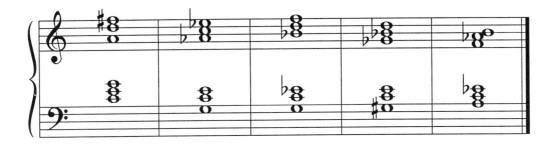

The above polytriads are created by combining any two triads at random. In order for these chords to be identifiable as polytriads, each triad must be played in a separate register, since were the notes to cross each other (the notes of one triad were played within the register of the other), each triad would no longer be discernible.

Experimenting with different registers and the spacing within each triad radically alters the sonority of each chord. In the following example, the lower triads are played in open-position while the upper triads are played in various inversions some with doubled outer-notes:

Figure 11-3

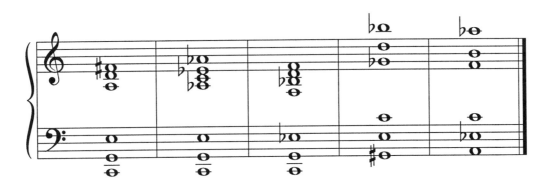

MUSICAL EXAMPLES

1) Triads can be used to harmonize or **shadow** a melodic phrase. In the following example, triads are played in closed-position in various inversions over an open-position pedal triad in the bass:

Figure 11-4

2) Alternatively, both triads can move independently to create a form of **polytriadic** harmony. In the following example, two major triads move in contrary motion—the left-hand triads are in second inversion and the right-hand triads are in root position:

Figure 11-5

3) In the final example, second inversion triads with doubled outer-notes in the right hand are shown above open-position triads in the left hand, producing rich and sonorous polytriadic harmonies:

Figure 11-6

Please note the following:

• The **clear grouping** of each triad is an essential feature of polytriadic harmony. If the notes of each triad merge or cross into each other's register, the triads will no longer be discernible.

• Notes from each triad can coincide (can be played as a unison or an octave), providing that the clear grouping of the notes of each triad is maintained.

• The sonority of a polytriad changes dramatically according to the register and inversion of the triads chosen. Polytriads sound particularly sonorous when closed-position triads are chosen for the upper part, and open-position triads are chosen for the lower part, as shown in **Figure 11-6**.

• A **polytriad** is a combination of two or more triads, a **polychord** is the generic term for a combination of two or more chords including triads. **Polytonality** occurs when two or more melodic lines move independently pertaining to two different keys centres.

• In jazz, polychordal harmony can be heard in the music of Duke Ellington, Gil Evans, George Russell and Dave Brubeck. These composers and arrangers were themselves influenced by 20th century classical composers; in particular Igor Stravinsky, Arnold Schoenberg, Alexander Skryabin, Claude Debussy, Darius Milhaud, Arthur Honegger, Béla Bartòk, Paul Hindemith, William Schuman, Charles Ives and Olivier Messiaen.

UPPER-STRUCTURE TRIADS

Polychords can also be formed by super-imposing triads above primary and secondary jazz chords. In jazz harmony, a triad played in this way is referred to as an **upper-structure**, while the chord base consisting of chord tones (tonic, third, fifth and seventh) is referred to as a **lower-structure**:

Figure 11-7

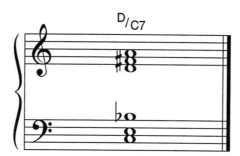

DOMINANT SEVENTH CHORDS

When building polytriads, all combinations can be considered musically interesting, each displaying a unique "tension" or "resonance". When polytriadic structures are introduced into jazz harmonic progressions, many combinations will prove too dissonant to be musically useful. An approach must therefore be adopted for selecting those upper-structures that function best within our existing harmonic system.

When adding extension intervals above dominant seventh chords, we learned that the **perfect fourth** and **major seventh** were consistently **dissonant** with the chord base. This also applies to upper-structure triads:

In the following examples, major, minor, augmented and diminished triads are shown for each degree of the chromatic scale, played over a C dominant seventh chord base. The triads in black contain either a perfect fourth [F] or major seventh [B], these triads are clearly too dissonant to be musically effective within our existing harmonic system:

Upper-Structure Major Triads:

Figure 11-8

Upper-Structure Minor Triads:

Figure 11-9

Upper-Structure Diminished Triads:

Figure 11-10

Upper-Structure Augmented Triads:

Figure 11-11

Each of the previous examples show the triad in root position, but they could as also have been shown in **first** or **second inversion**, and with one of the **outer notes doubled**. Furthermore, the bass note could be played by a bass player or else omitted, depending on the musical context:

Figure 11-12

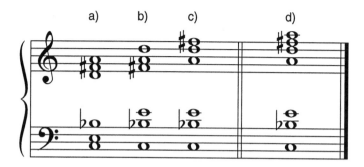

a) Root Position
b) First Inversion
c) Second Inversion
d) Second Inversion with fifth doubled at the octave

Please note the following:

• The chord shown in **Figure 11-12** can be symbolized in one of two ways:

a) as **D/C7** suggesting a D triad over C7 chord,

b) as **C7$^{\#11}$**, or **C7$^{9/\#11}$**, or **C9$^{\#11}$**.

Shown below are some of the most frequently used upper-structures for dominant seventh chords. Each example is followed by a **key** that includes both the chord symbol and the degree of the scale on which each triad is built:

Upper-Structure Major Triads:

Figure 11-13

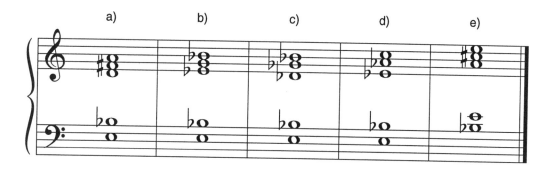

Key: **Degree of the scale:**

a) C7#11 or C7#11/13   -   II
b) C7+9   -   bIII
c) C7b9/#11   -   bV
d) C7#9/b13 or C7 alt   -   bVI
e) C7b9   -   VI

Upper-Structure Minor Triads:

Figure 11-14

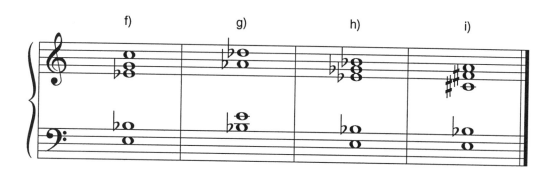

Key: **Degree of the scale:**

f) C7+9   -   Im
g) C7b9/b13 or C7alt   -   bIIm
h) C7#9/#11   -   bIIIm
i) C7b9/#11   -   #IVm

Upper-Structure Diminished Triads:

Figure 11-15

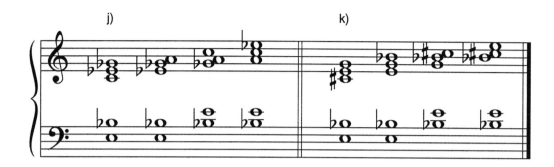

Key: **Degrees of the scale:**

j) C7♭9/♯11, C7♭9/13   -   Idim, ♭IIIdim, ♭Vdim, VIdim
k) C7♭9   -   ♭IIdim, IIIdim, Vdim, ♭VIIdim

Upper-Structure Augmented Triads:

Figure 11-16

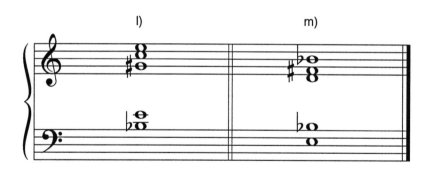

Key: **Degree of the scale:**

l) C7aug, C+7, C7♭13   -   Iaug
m) C7♯11   -   IIaug

Exercise:

Having practiced these chords for C7, explore alternative inversions and doublings as shown in **Figure 11-12**, and then transpose them into all twelve keys.

MINOR SEVENTH CHORDS

The process of super-imposing triads can be extended to minor seventh chords. As with all extension intervals, many dissonances will occur if triads are freely imposed above the minor chord base. One effective approach is to use only those triads found in the **Dorian Minor Scale**. The Dorian minor scale, or Dorian mode, contains a minor third, minor sixth and minor seventh, and is the same as the major scale of which it is the second degree.

In the following example, G Dorian minor scale is shown, which contains the same notes as F major scale:

Figure 11-17

The G minor seventh chord is the II of a II-V-I cadence in F. Seven triads built on each degree of the scale can be shown as follows:

Figure 11-18

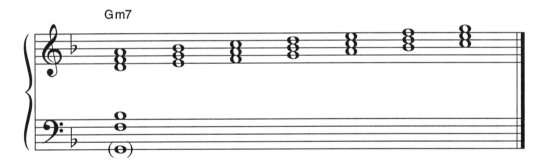

Shown below are some of the polychords that can be derived from the G Dorian minor scale. Upper-structure triads can be played in various inversions and with notes doubled. Notice how the fifth is sometimes introduced between the third and seventh to give the left-hand chord added stability and weight, particularly when the bass note is omitted:

Figure 11-19

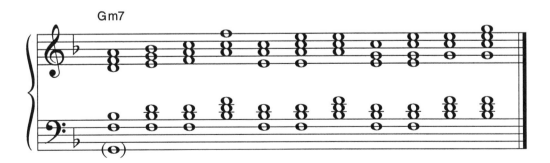

MAJOR SEVENTH CHORDS

The process of super-imposing triads can be extended to the major sevenths. To avert the dissonance of the fourth, triads found derived from the **Lydian Major Scale** are shown. The Lydian major mode, or Lydian mode, contains a major third and an augmented fourth, and is the same as the major scale of which it is the fourth degree.

In the following example, F Lydian major scale is shown, which contains the same notes as C major scale:

Figure 11-20

The F Lydian major seventh chord is the I of a II-V-I cadence in F. Seven triads built on each degree of the scale can be shown as follows:

Figure 11-21

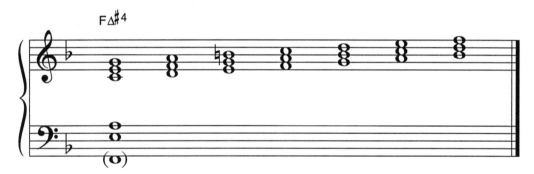

The *lydianisation* of major scales is a device often used by jazz musicians to avert the dissonance that normally arises between the major third and the fourth of the scale. Shown below are some of the polychords that can be derived from the F Lydian major scale. Again, the fifth is introduced between the third and seventh to give the left-hand chord added stability and weight, particularly when the bass note is omitted. Finally, a triad built on the V of the scale (C) can be played over a sixth chord as an alternatives for the I chord:

Figure 11-22

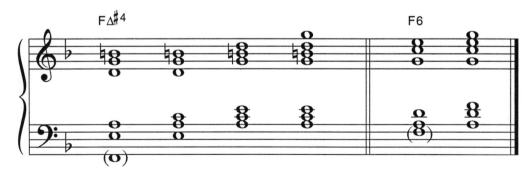

II-V-I CADENCES AND UPPER-STRUCTURE TRIADS

We have learned how triads can be super-imposed above each chord in a II-V-I cadence. Clearly there are many possibilities for upper-structures above dominant seventh chords (V), whereas the possibilities for minor seventh (II) and major seventh chords (I) are more limited. To compensate for this, we shall introduce some non-triadic upper-structure triads for minor seventh and major seventh chords, including minor eleventh, major sixth chords.

Outlined below is a glossary of II-V-I cadences that use upper-structures in various combinations. After playing each example, analyse it to fully understand its harmonic structure and then transpose it into other keys. You may find it helpful to play the bass note after each chord has sounded, so that the full harmony can be heard:

Figure 11-23

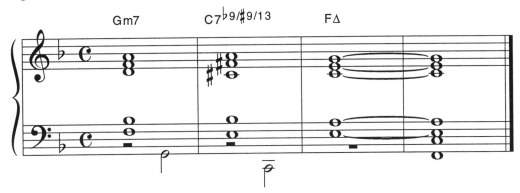

Figure 11-24

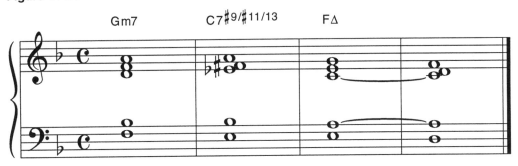

Figure 11-25

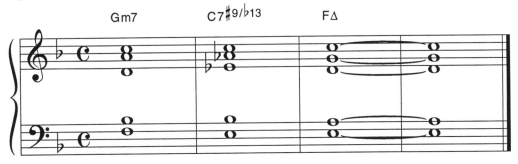

Figure 11-26

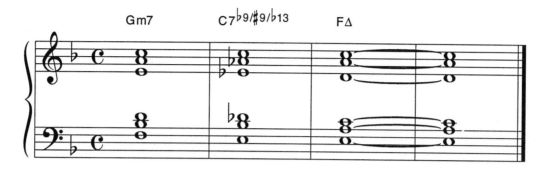

Figure 11-27

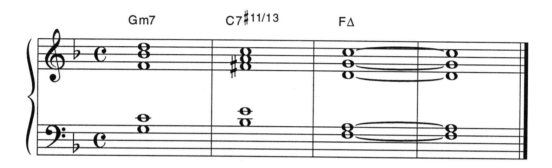

Figure 11-28

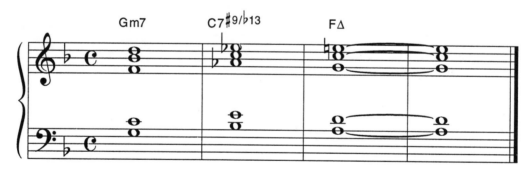

Figure 11-29

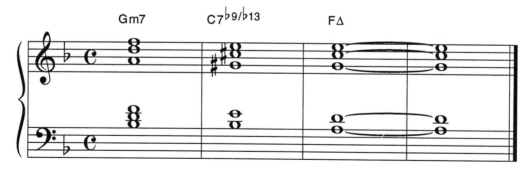

Figure 11-30

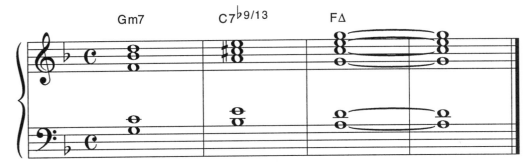

Figure 11-31

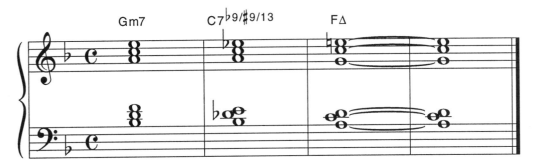

Figure 11-32

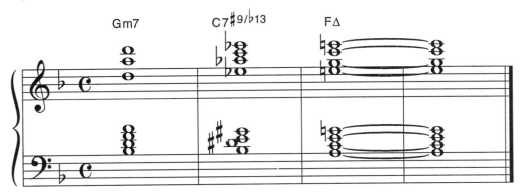

MUSICAL EXAMPLES

An upper-structures can be used to **emphasize** the melody. Furthermore, the melody can be transposed up an octave to provide sufficient space for the accompanying chords.

In the first example, the opening phrase of "Stella by Starlight" is transposed up an octave for a more "dramatic" exclamation of the theme. Notice that the bass notes are played during the held chords, the sustain pedal can be used to mask any breaks in the harmonic line:

Figure 11-33

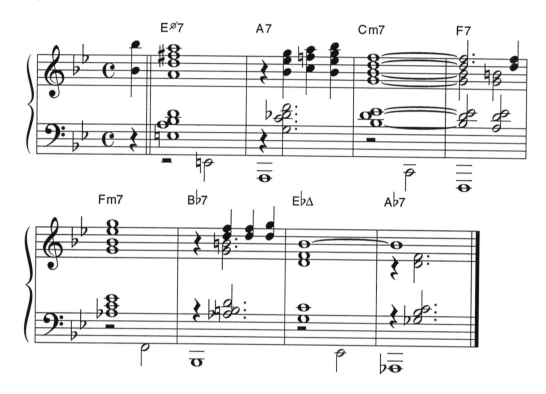

The first four bars of "It's Easy To Remember" can also be transposed up an octave. In the following example, bass notes have been omitted to create a "floating" effect:

Figure 11-34

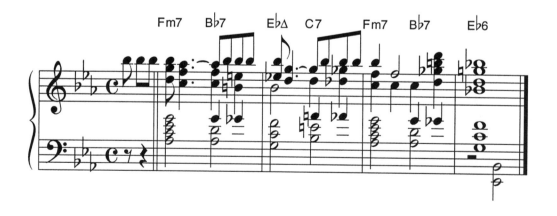

In the final example, the opening phrase of "If I Should Lose You" is shown. First two bars are played in the original register, while the repetition of the phrase in bars 3 and 4 is played up and octave. This is immediately followed by a return to the original register with some highly dense harmony in the last two bars:

Figure 11-35

Please note the following:

• The musical examples shown in this chapter demonstrate how triads can be super-imposed above a chord base to create dynamic and dense chordal structures. This works musically because of the inherent properties of the triad creates *polychordal* effect.

• When playing chords with so many parts, it is not always possible to adhere strictly to the voice-leading principles shown in previous chapters. Furthermore, a decisive break in the harmonic line can be used for dramatic effect.

• It should also be reiterated that it is not the jazz pianist's aim to play the densest and most complex harmony possible, but rather to acquire the facility to move freely between highly dense and sparse chordal structures, depending on the musical narrative. When accompanying, we should be sensitive to the needs of other instrumentalists and vocalists, and to not "overplay" the chords. As with all good music making, the "proximity of silence" and knowing "what to leave out" should be guiding principles.

CHAPTER TWELVE

BLOCK CHORDS

In this chapter, we shall use the primary and secondary jazz chords to create **block chords**, and see how they form the harmonic basis of the **locked-hand style** most often associated with the pianist George Shearing. Block chords, **four-way close** and **drop two voicings** are all commonly found in arrangements for big bands and jazz combos.

THE LOCKED-HAND STYLE

In the following example, the opening of "Easy Living" is shown in a **locked-hand style**:

Figure 12-1

In **Figure 12-1**, the melody is accompanied by block chords, it is also **doubled** as a single legato line an octave lower in the left-hand, giving it a deeper resonance.   The bass notes could have been played during breaks in the melodic line, but since every note of the melody is **harmonized**, it makes the bass line less imperative.

HARMONIC BASIS OF THE LOCKED-HAND STYLE

To play in a **locked-hand style** means to "shadow" a melodic line with an underlying progression of chords. It is usually a feature of trio or combo playing where the bass line is given over to a bassist, leaving both hands free to play the melody and chords in a more rhythmic way. The style can be used both when playing within a group and when playing solo. Many jazz pianists have incorporated the style into their playing, including Earl Hines, Oscar Peterson, Erroll Garner, Wynton Kelly, Barry Harris and Kenny Barron, but for the purposes of this book we shall examine the style developed by **George Shearing** in the 50's. To fully appreciate how the locked-hand style is actually played by jazz pianists, it is essential to listen to the classic recordings by Shearing and others.

The **primary** and **secondary jazz chords** form the harmonic basis of the locked-hand style, rather than the three, four and five-part chords shown in previous chapters. The most important chords are as follows:

1) The **major sixth** chord (played in preference to the major seventh)
2) The **minor sixth** chord
3) The **minor seventh** chord
4) The **dominant seventh** chord
5) The **half-diminished seventh** chord
6) The **diminished seventh** chord

• The above chords can also be **inverted** to form first, second and third inversions:

Figure 12-2

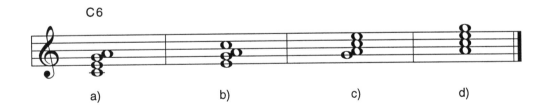

a) In **root** position
b) In **first** inversion
c) In **second** inversion
d) In **third** inversion

FOUR-WAY CLOSE

The first two bars of **Figure 12-1** uses inversions of the accompanying chords to shadow the melody, this is possible because the melody consists only of chord tones: F6 (in place of F•), F#°7, Gm7 and G#°7. However, in bar 3 the first two melody notes are not present in the accompanying chord (F6), to harmonize these notes a **diminished seventh** chord is used. This refers to a harmonic device called **four-way close**.

Four-way close is a device used by composers and arrangers to harmonize scale passages that include notes that are not chord tones. To harmonize each degree of a major scale the accompanying chords must alternate between inversions of the base chord and inversions of a diminished seventh chord. A **chromatic passing note** will also be needed to create an **eight-note** scale.

The C major scale can be harmonized by alternating between closed-position voicings of the C6 chord and a diminished seventh chord. The diminished seventh chord of F, Ab, B and D all refer to the same chord in different inversions and are played between each C6 chord to produced a smooth harmonization of the scale. Notice that a chromatic passing note [Ab] has been introduced between the fifth and sixth degree of the scale:

Figure 12-3

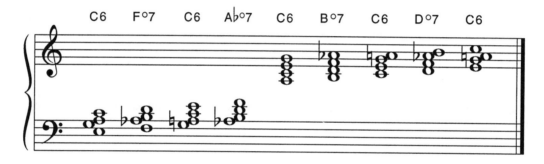

The progression could also be interpreted as a succession of V-I cadences in C, since the diminished seventh chord functions as a **rootless** dominant seventh chord (G7) with a flattened ninth:

Example 12-1

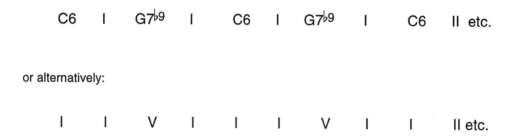

or alternatively:

| I | I | V | I | I | I | V | I | I | II etc. |

DIMINISHED SEVENTH CHORDS

Diminished seventh chords are **symmetrical** chords: that is to say they consist of three equal intervals (minor thirds) stacked on top of one another, dividing the octave into four equal parts. Transposing a diminished seventh chord up or down by a minor third will result in a chord containing exactly the same notes (as shown in **Figure 12-3**). There are only **three** diminished seventh chords, each one consisting of the same notes:

Figure 12-4

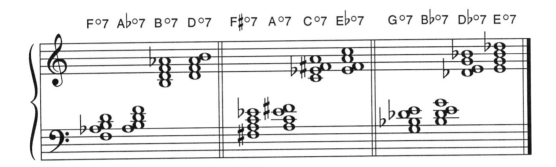

FOUR-WAY CLOSE PROGRESSIONS

Shown below are the four-way close progressions for major sixth, minor sixth, minor seventh, dominant seventh, half-diminished and diminished seventh chords. Notice that four notes are taken in the right-hand and one note in the left-hand; this enables the lower part to be played legato, creating a particularly deep sonority. The six scales should be practiced as written and then transposed into all keys:

Major sixth chords, four-way close:

Figure 12-5

Minor sixth chords, four-way close:

Figure 12-6

Minor seventh chords, four-way close:

Figure 12-7

Dominant seventh chords, four-way close:

Figure 12-8

Half-diminished seventh chords, four-way close:

Figure 12-9

Diminished seventh chords, four-way close:

Figure 12-10

Please note the following:

• The chromatic passing note for **major** and **minor sixth** scales is the **flattened sixth**:

Figure 12-11

• The chromatic passing note for **minor** and **dominant seventh** scales is the **major seventh**:

Figure 12-12

Useful Tip:

• To find the correct alternating chord to play four-way close, select the diminished seventh chord that begins on the **second degree** of the scale.

For example: to play four-way close for an F6 scale, G diminished seventh chord is the correct alternating chord (G°7, Bb°7, Db°7 and E°7):

Figure 12-13

DROP TWO VOICINGS

By transposing down by an octave the second note from the top of each chord, the chords can be rearranged and played in **open-position**. These are referred to as **drop two** voicings since it is the second note from the top that is "dropped" Any of the notes of the closed-position chord can be transposed in this way, but the second note from the top is the most widely used by composers and arrangers:

Figure 12-14

Exercises:

i) Play major sixth, minor sixth, minor seventh, dominant seventh, half-diminished and diminished seventh chords, ascending and descending the keyboard as drop two voicings.

ii) Practice the same chords in all keys.

DROP TWO, FOUR-WAY CLOSE

Having fully understood the workings of four-way close and played drop two voicings in all keys, the two can be combined to form **drop two, four-way close** progressions.

Outlined below are the progressions for major sixth, minor sixth, minor seventh, dominant seventh, half-diminished and diminished seventh chords:

Major sixth chords, drop two, four-way close:

Figure 12-15

Minor sixth chords, drop two, four-way close:

Figure 12-16

Minor seventh chords, drop two, four-way close:

Figure 12-17

Dominant seventh chords, drop two, four-way close:

Figure 12-18

Half-diminished seventh chords, drop two, four-way close:

Figure 12-19

Diminished seventh chords, drop two, four-way close:

Figure 12-20

MAJOR SEVENTH DROP TWO, FOUR WAY CLOSE

The major seventh chord is less often played as a block chord due to the dissonance that exists between the major seventh and the tonic. The dissonance is particularly acute when played as a drop two chord in third inversion, with the major seventh at the bottom of the chord. However, the other inversions, including root position, can be freely used:

Figure 12-21

OTHER FEATURES OF THE LOCKED-HAND STYLE

Outlined below are some additional features of the locked-hand style:

1) When playing minor seventh and dominant seventh block chords in closed-position, the **ninth** can be played instead of the tonic. In the following example, Cm7 and C7 chords are played with the ninth instead of the tonic:

Figure 12-22

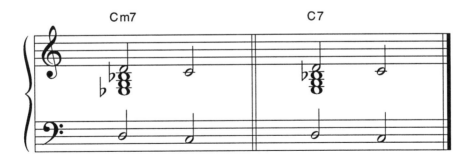

2) If a dominant seventh voicing were played with a **flattened** ninth and with the tonic omitted, the resultant chord would be identical to a diminished seventh chord a semitone above:

Figure 12-23

3) The diminished or octatonic scale consists of an alternation of **steps** and **half-steps**, and can be effectively used as the basis for harmonic patterns on dominant seventh chords:

Figure 12-24

By holding the bottom two notes of the diminished seventh chord constant and approaching the upper two notes by a tone shift *downwards*, an effective harmonic pattern can be created. Remember that the same diminished seventh chord can be played for four different keys:

Figure 12-25

4) This diminished seventh pattern shown in **Figure 12-25** might typically be used to harmonize a melody descending the natural minor scale during the V chord in a II-V-I cadence:

Figure 12-26

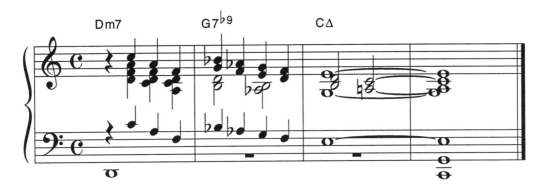

5) Finally, George Shearing liked to decorate the left-hand line by introducing **grace notes** to emphasize the melody. He also stressed the left-hand melody by giving it a little more weight and substance than the right-hand chords above:

Figure 12-27

MUSICAL EXAMPLES

In the first example, the opening of "Easy Living" is shown, this time with **drop two** voicings:

Figure 12-28

The opening of "If I Should Lose You" features a repeat of the same melodic phrase. **Diminished scale harmony** is introduced in the second D7 chord:

Figure 12-29

There are occasions when it makes sense to play a chord once to accompany several melody notes. The opening passage of "Out of Nowhere" features four ascending eighth notes, the chord once at the beginning of the phrase and once at the end:

Figure 12-30

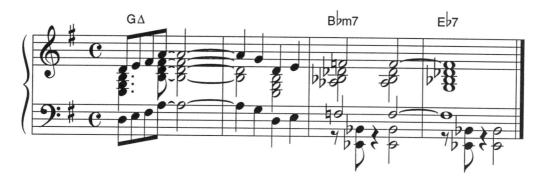

Finally, the opening passage of Harold Arlen and Johnny Mercer's "That Old Black Magic" is shown. It presents a difficulty for the solo jazz pianist - what to do when bar after bar is based on the same harmony? One solution is to use block chords to emphasize the melody and introduce some syncopation:

Figure 12-31

CHAPTER THIRTEEN

PENTATONIC HARMONY

In this chapter, we shall introduce **pentatonic harmony**, and see how it can form the basis of **quartal** and **quintal voicings**. Pentatonic scales were crucial to both the melodic and harmonic development of jazz, and can be heard in the playing of many contemporary jazz pianists.

PENTATONIC SCALES

The three pentatonic scales used in jazz are as follows:

Major Pentatonic Scale:

Figure 13-1

The **C major pentatonic scale** consist of the first, second, third, fifth and sixth degrees of the major scale. The omitted intervals are the perfect fourth and major seventh that are dissonant when played against a major triad.

Minor Pentatonic Scale:

Figure 13-2

The **C minor pentatonic scale** consist of the same notes as the *relative major* pentatonic scale. In the previous example, C minor is the relative minor of E♭ major, consequently the pentatonic scale of C minor consists of the same notes as E♭ major pentatonic scale.

C Dorian Minor Pentatonic Scale:

Figure 13-3

The **C Dorian minor pentatonic** scale is the same as the major pentatonic scale but with a *minor* third. The term "Dorian" is used because the scale contains a minor third and a major sixth, in accordance with the Dorian mode.

Please note the following:

• There are twelve major and twelve minor pentatonic scales, the minor pentatonic scales are derived from the major pentatonic scale. There are also twelve Dorian minor pentatonic scales that are a hybrid of the major and minor pentatonic scales. In all keys there are a total of **24 scales**.

• The word "pentatonic" means "five tones," and is derived from the Greek word "penta" meaning "five" and "tonic" meaning "tones."

QUARTAL VOICINGS

In the same way that notes of a major scale can be stacked in thirds to produce triads and seventh chords, the notes of a **pentatonic scale** can be stacked in fourths (or fifths) to produce **quartal voicings**. The most convenient way to do this is to begin with the tonic note [C] and place each alternate note of the pentatonic scale *downwards* until all five notes have sounded. Notice that the resultant chord is made up entirely of fourths:

Figure 13-4

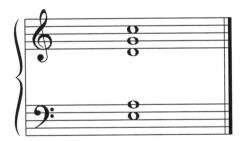

Alternatively, we can begin with the tonic note [C] and place every third note of the pentatonic scale *upwards* until all five notes have sounded. Notice that the resultant chord is made up entirely of fifths:

Figure 13-5

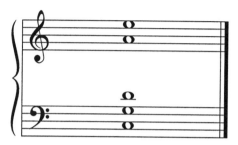

INVERTED QUARTAL VOICINGS

The quartal voicing shown in **Figure 13-4** can also be inverted in the same way as triads and seventh chords. The following chords should be practiced in all keys:

Major Pentatonic Chord with inversions

Figure 13-6

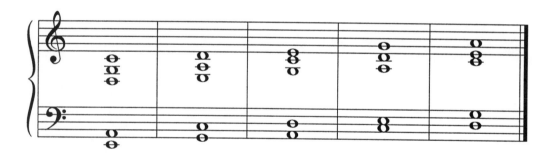

Minor Pentatonic Chord with inversions

Figure 13-7

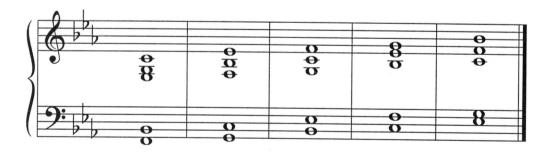

Dorian Minor Pentatonic Chord with inversions

Figure 13-8

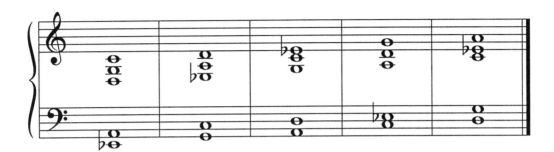

MUSICAL APPLICATION

We have already seen that major seventh chords and major sixth chords are fairly interchangeable in most situations. If the melody note should fall on either the tonic, second, third, fifth or sixth during a major seventh or sixth chord, it should be possible to harmonize using inversions of a major pentatonic chord, as shown in **Figure 13-6**.

In the following melodic extract, the melodic line in the first bar consists entirely of notes found in the C major pentatonic scale, it can be harmonized using notes of the C pentatonic scale:

Figure 13-9

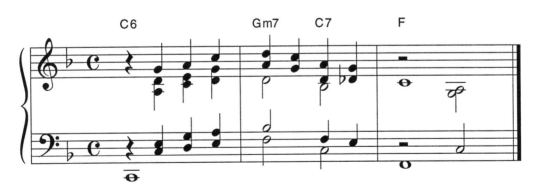

In the second bar, the first two beats consist entirely of notes found in the G minor pentatonic scale, therefore the melody can be harmonized using notes of the G minor pentatonic scale:

Figure 13-10

II-V-I CADENCES AND QUARTAL VOICINGS

In **major** and **minor II-V-I cadences**, quartal voicings are most often played in place of the II and V chords. The following patterns should be practiced in all keys:

Figure 13-11

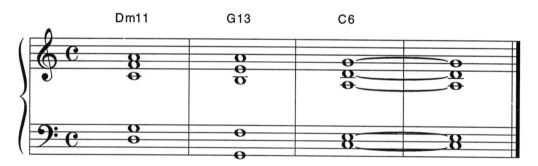

Figure 13-12

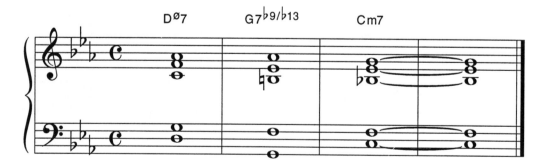

PLAYING WITH QUARTAL VOICINGS

Chromatic Motion:

Quartal voicings can be played *ascending* and *descending* the **chromatic** scale:

Figure 13-13

In the following example, pentatonic chords are shown shadowing a melodic line:

Figure 13-14

Please note the following:

• It is a feature of all chords derived from pentatonic scales that they pertain to a particular key or tonal centre, this is because they contain notes that are only consonant with the triad. For example, the C major pentatonic chord clearly defines the tonality of C major since the added intervals to the triad are the second (D) and sixth (A), both of which are consonant intervals in the C major scale.

• Pentatonic chords can be used to shadow a melodic line in a similar way to the **polytriadic harmony** shown in *Chapter Eleven*.

Diatonic Motion:

Quartal voicings can also be played *ascending* or *descending* a **diatonic** scale (major scale). Since all diatonic scales contain a combination of both steps and half steps, the intervals within each voicing will need to change in accordance to the scale.

In the following example, a quartal voicing is shown ascending the C major scale:

Figure 13-15

If the same chords were played over a D in the bass, they would be in the **Dorian Mode** of D:

Figure 13-16

Please note the following:

• We first became aware of the significance of the Dorian mode in jazz in *Chapter Eleven*, when upper-structure triads derived from the Dorian mode were shown above the chord base of the II chord in a II-V-I Cadence. Quartal voicings in the Dorian mode produces what are often referred to as "So What" chords in jazz, referring to the tune of the same name that appeared on Miles Davis' legendary album *Kind of Blue* in the late 50's. This record more than any other helped to establish **modal jazz**. The Dorian mode provided the harmonic basis for many of the tunes, as well as the voicings played on the album by the pianist Bill Evans.

Shown here is the "riff" or "head" from Miles Davis' *So What:*

Figure 13-17

PENTATONIC SUBSTITUTION CHORDS

Once all twenty-four pentatonic chords and their inversions have been fully learned in all keys, they can then be played as **substitution** chords in place of standard chords in harmonic progressions. For example, where a C major seventh chord is symbolized, as well as C pentatonic chords, G pentatonic chords can be played.

Shown below are quintal voicings in keys pertaining to their substitution function in jazz chord progressions:

1) **CΔ, C6** - play **C major pentatonic** chords:

Figure 13-18

2) C△ - play **G major pentatonic** chords:

Figure 13-19

3) C△**#4** - play **D major pentatonic** chords:

Figure 13-20

4) **Cm7** - play **Eb major pentatonic** chords:

Figure 13-21

5) **Cm6, Cm7** - play **C Dorian minor pentatonic** chords:

Figure 13-22

6) **C⌀7 (Cm7♭5)** - play **E♭ Dorian minor pentatonic** chords:

Figure 13-23

7) **C7, C9, C13** - play **G Dorian minor pentatonic** chords:

Figure 13-24

8) **C7alt** - play **G♭ major pentatonic** chords:

Figure 13-25

9) **Csus** - play **F major pentatonic** chords:

Figure 13-26

10) **C7sus4 (C7sus)** - play **B♭ major pentatonic** chords:

Figure 13-27

QUINTAL VOICINGS

A chord consisting only of fourths *descending* from the tonic contains the same notes as a chord consisting of fifths *ascending* from the tonic (**Figures 13-4** and **13-5**). **Quintal voicings** sound very sonorous on the piano, particularly in the lower register of the keyboard. The pianist and composer Duke Ellington liked to play the following voicings:

Figure 13-28

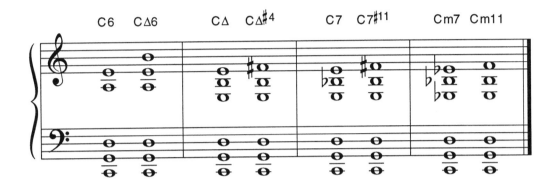

MUSICAL EXAMPLES

Shown here are arrangements of standard songs that include quartal or quintal voicings.

In the first example, the opening phrase of "Out Of Nowhere" is harmonized using quartal voicings. Open fifths are played in the bass during held notes:

Figure 13-29

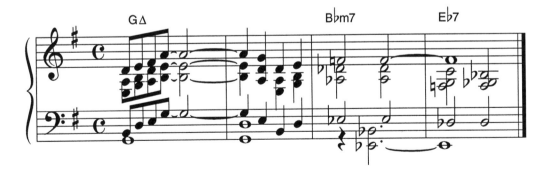

The first four notes of "My Ideal" are based on the pentatonic scale and are harmonized using quartal voicings. In bar 4 a quintal voicing is used to create a final sounding chord:

Figure 13-30

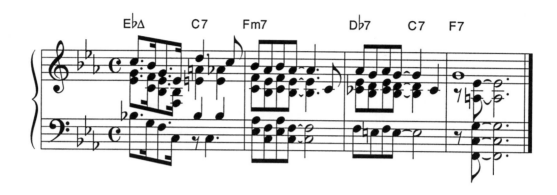

The bridge passage of "Easy Living" features a sizeable shift in register for the triplet figure in bar 2. In the following example, the triplet figure is shadowed by quartal voicings moving in **chromatic** motion:

Figure 13-31

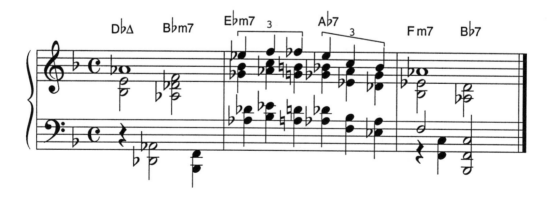

Finally, the opening phrase of "It's Easy to Remember" is shown accompanied by quartal voicings. The voicing for the B♭7 chord in the first bar is derived from the tritone substitution chord of B♭7 (E7), played over its dominant (B). Tritone substitution appears again between the Fm7 and B♭7 chord in bar 3, followed by a chromatic approach into the last bar in contrary motion. The example concludes with a quintal voicing on the tonic chord:

Figure 13-32

Please note the following:

• Three, four, five and six-part chords can be formed using the notes of a pentatonic scale, they can also be inverted to produce a vast array of chordal shapes.

• Due to their harmonic structure they are ideally suited to harmonizing or shadowing a melodic line, this may involve either **chromatic** (or **parallel**) or **diatonic** motion.

• Having become familiar with the sound of quartal and quintal voicings, and become proficient at finding them in all keys, they can be gradually introduced as an alternative to primary and secondary jazz chords when playing standard harmonic progressions.

• Quartal and quintal voicings share many features, including their suitability for chromatic and diatonic motion. However, quintal voicings cannot be inverted, though they can be effectively arranged to form sonorous chords (**Figure 13-28**).

• It is interesting to note that the **interval** of a fifth (or fourth) forms the basis of the pentatonic scale, while the **cycle** of fifths forms the harmonic basis of standard jazz chord progressions.

Conclusion:

The pentatonic scale is fundamental to all western music. In jazz, the introduction of pentatonic harmony reached a high degree of sophistication in the music of the saxophonist John Coltrane and the pianist McCoy Tyner. Coltrane used pentatonic scales as the basis of a radically new melodic syntax, while Tyner used quartal voicings when accompanying. For a deeper understanding of the way quartal voicings can be used in jazz, listen to Coltrane's classic albums "A Love Supreme" and "My Favourite Things," and also to Tyner's "The Real McCoy."

CHAPTER FOURTEEN

ODDS & ENDS

In this chapter, we shall introduce some devices that fall outside of our harmonic system, such as **opening** and **final chords**, **partial** and **cluster voicings**, all of which can be played in our arrangements of standard songs.

OPENING AND FINAL CHORDS

The opening and final chord of a song may well be the tonic, it may also be symbolized as a plain major or minor triad (C instead of C•). This may be because the melody ends on the tonic and a major seventh interval in the chord would create a dissonance. Nevertheless, a more substantial sounding chord may often be desirable.

In the following example, the tonic and fifth are played in the left-hand, and the **ninth** is introduced adjacent to the third, creating a more substantial chord:

Figure 14-1

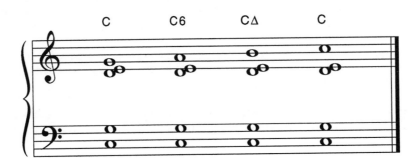

Please note the following:

• The chords shown in **Figure 14-1** could be played at any stage within a song, though to play the tonic and fifth in the bass for too many chords in succession would make the accompaniment sound too heavy.

• When the melody ends on the tonic note, a major sixth (C6) rather than a major seventh chord (CΔ) is usually indicated, this is to avert the dissonance that would occur between the major seventh interval and the melody note.

FURTHER VARIATIONS FOR THE II-V-I CADENCE

We have made a fairly exhaustive study of the II-V-I cadence and seen how it can be played in three, four, five and six parts, and with reharmonization. One further harmonic device is to **transpose** the notes within each chord to create more extreme tensions between the parts:

Consider the following II-V-I cadence:

Figure 14-2

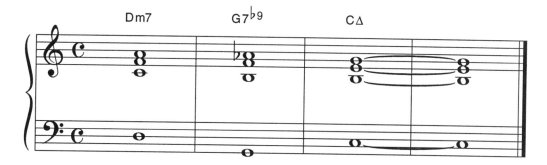

If we were to **transpose** the top part *down* by an octave, and the third part *up* by an octave, the following chords would be created:

Figure 14-3

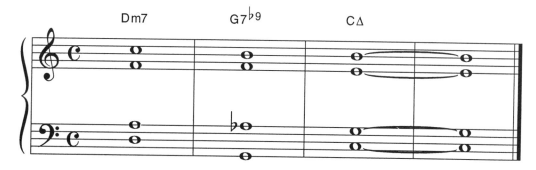

The process can also be applied to the alternative register of the II-V-I cadence. Shown first is the original II-V-I cadence:

Figure 14-4

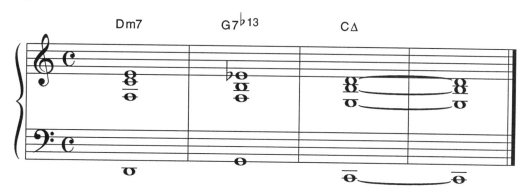

By transposing the top part *down* by an octave and the third part *up* by an octave, the following chords are created:

Figure 14-5

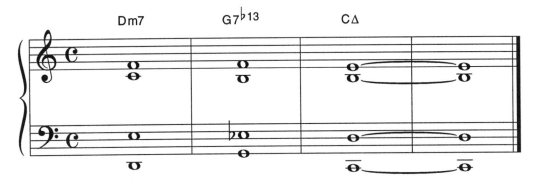

Reharmonization can also be introduced into the previous examples. In the following example, **Figure 14-3** is shown with a minor-major substitution on chord II, a suspension on chord V, and a major seventh to sixth resolution on chord I:

Figure 14-6

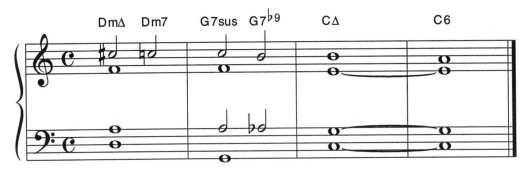

Alternatively, **Figure 14-5** can be reharmonized as follows:

Figure 14-7

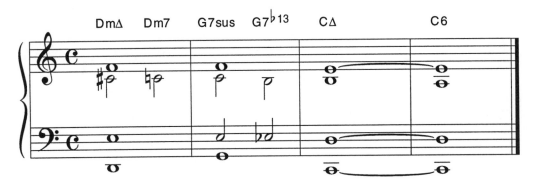

The musical effect of transposing the constituent parts of a chord may well depend on the register. Listen to how different **Figure 14-7** sounds when played in the key of G major, together with a **chromatic approach** in the tenor line to the II and I chord of the cadence:

Figure 14-8

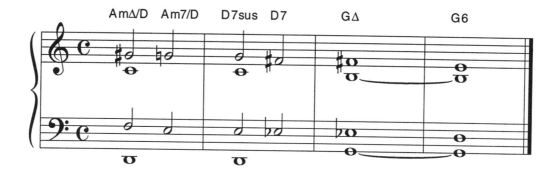

PARTIAL VOICINGS

All the chords we have played so far have consisted of a tonic, third and seventh, together with optional fourth, fifth and sixth parts. Having learned how to manipulate these chordal structures while observing voice-leading principles, we shall direct this knowledge towards creating some lighter-sounding voicings. These **partial voicings** will also introduce a degree of "ambiguity" into our harmonic system.

In the following example, a Dm9 chord is shown, but this time the seventh has been omitted. Since the rest of the chord clearly defines the harmony, the harmonic ambiguity created by the absence of the seventh produces a lighter-sounding voicing:

Figure 14-9

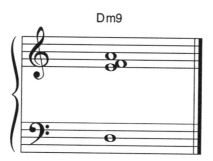

Partial voicings can be created for all primary and secondary jazz chords, though the presence of the third remains fairly crucial to defining the chord. Shown here are some evocative partial voicings for the three chords in a II-V-I cadence:

Minor Seventh Chords:

Figure 14-10

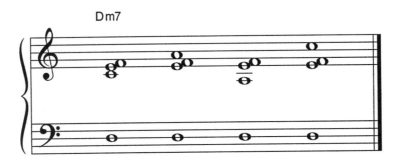

Dominant Seventh Chords:

Figure 14-11

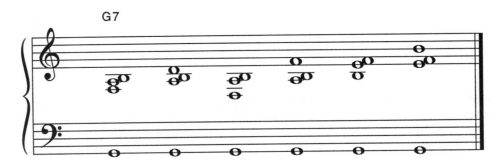

Major Seventh Chords:

Figure 14-12

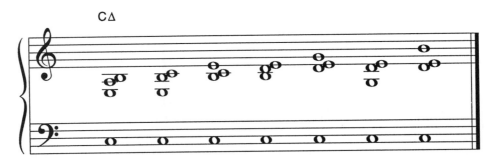

Please note the following:

• The partial voicings shown here place the third and ninth adjacent to each other, giving each voicing a particularly "crunchy" sound.

• The **third** is the most crucial interval, since in a harmonic progression it is the third that will define each chord as being either major or minor. The other intervals (tonic, fifth and seventh) define the harmony more emphatically. In the examples shown, the third is always present, whereas the tonic, fifth or seventh may be omitted.

• Partial voicings create a "floating" and "suggestive" harmony, one that can be directly attributed to the harmonic approach adopted by French "impressionist" composers of the 1900s (Claude Debussy, Maurice Ravel and Erik Satie). The jazz pianist Bill Evans created a unique harmonic concept by welding this harmonic approach with the language of jazz.

• Partial voicings also sound effective when played on an electric piano or synthesizer.

CLUSTER VOICINGS

We have seen that by omitting one or more intervals from a closed-position voicing, a lighter and more harmonically ambiguous voicing is created. This process can now be extended to produce all kinds of chordal shapes. **Cluster voicings** are created by freely combining chord tones with extension intervals to create new and evocative sonorities irrespective of the order in which they are played; an analogy could be made between "cluster voicings" in music and "splashes of colour" in painting. This process works most effectively when notes from a fixed scale are chosen, one that relates directly to the chord being played.

For example: we have learned that Dm7 is the II in a II-V-I cadence in C, and that the **Dorian mode** can be used to produce upper-structures since it contains the same notes as the C major scale. The Dorian mode can also be shown as a chord by stacking thirds in accordance to the scale:

Figure 14-13

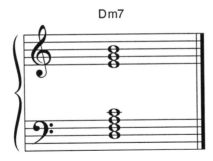

In the following example, the chord tones of Dm7 are freely combined with extension intervals derived from the Dorian mode (ninth, eleventh and thirteenth) to produce a broad array of chordal shapes:

In the **lower** register:

Figure 14-14

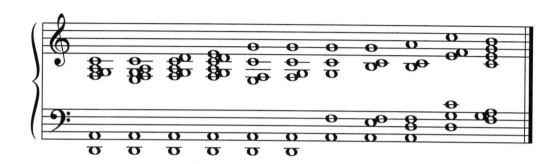

In the **higher** register:

Figure 14-15

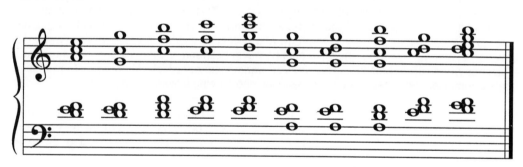

In the following example, a C7 chord is shown as stacked thirds with several extension intervals:

Figure 14-16

The above chord contains notes that are all found within the following **diminished scale**:

Figure 14-17

Consequently, the following cluster voicings can be created by freely combining the chord tones with extension intervals:

Figure 14-18

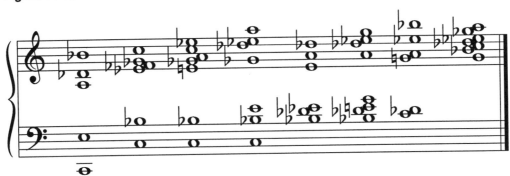

ARPEGGIATING THE LEFT-HAND

Finally, a useful pianistic device to use when some harmonic motion needed during held note or a break in the melodic line. **Arpeggiation** beginning with the chord tones in the left-hand helps to "stagger" the impact of each new chord.

In the following example, a D minor seventh chord is arpeggiated in the left-hand:

Figure 14-19

Arpeggiation of the left-hand can also be used continuously to form a florid accompaniment to held chords in the right-hand, Bill Evans used this device extensively when playing solo:

Figure 14-20

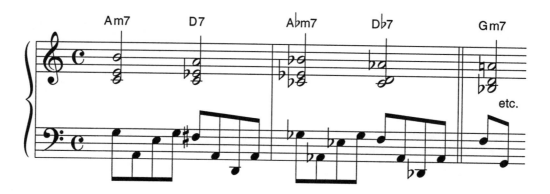

CONCLUSION

The key to playing really good jazz piano is firstly, to acquire a familiarity with the jazz piano idiom, this can only be brought about by going to live performances and listening extensively to original recordings; secondly, key literacy is a prerequisite to thoroughly learning the keyboard and to be able to reproduce simple melodic phrases chords in all keys. This process can best be achieved by practicing what you know already in all keys. This is also a good time to begin compiling your own glossary of musical "discoveries."

CHAPTER FIFTEEN

THE INFLUENCE OF CLASSICAL PIANO

In this final chapter, we shall highlight the enormous influence the classical piano repertoire has had on jazz pianists. This can clearly be heard in the playing of Art Tatum, Oscar Peterson, Bill Evans, Herbie Hancock, Chick Corea, Keith Jarrett and many others. It is an enormous subject, though certain elements can be easily assimilated to expand our vocabulary of useful pianistic devices. Furthermore, the process should help to engender a greater awareness of the many connections between the two musical idioms.

HYMNS

By way of an introduction to classical harmony, the purchase of a **hymnbook** is essential. Hymns were composed to accompany sacred "poems" and are typically eight, ten, twelve or sixteen bars long. Reproduced here is the hymn *At the Name of Jesus* by W. H. Monk (1823-89), a gem of both melodic and harmonic construction:

Figure 15-1

Synopsis:

• The above hymn is in four parts and consists mainly of **major** and **minor** triads. Since a triad contains only three notes, one note must be *doubled* to form a fourth part: this is usually the tonic or the fifth, but occasionally the third.

• Harmonic variation is achieved by introducing **inversions** (first and second inversions), **passing notes** (half-note or whole-note passages to "break up" the harmonic rhythm), **modulation** (changing to different keys), or **extension intervals** (sixths, ninths etc.).

• In classical theory, there are four principal **cadences: perfect** (V to I); **imperfect** (anything to V); **plagal** (IV to I); **interrupted** (V to anything except I). Each four-bar phrase normally concludes with one of these cadencial formulas.

• In classical theory, there are three principal **suspensions:** from **2 to 1** (supertonic to tonic); from **4 to 3** (sub-dominant to third); from **6 to 5** (from submediant to perfect fifth). Chords that appear which are not conventional triads may well be suspensions, in such cases by looking at the chords that follow will help to deduce the suspension.

• When **accidentals** appear (sharps and flats), it probably involves modulating into another key. **Modulation** usually occurs by means of a perfect cadence in the new key. Remember that the dominant chord (V) in both major and minor perfect cadences is always major, and that accidentals will invariably appear at the point of modulation, which is the dominant chord of the new key. For example; in bar 6 of **Figure 15-1**, an A♯ appears in the bass: A♯ is the major third of F♯ major and is the V chord of the new key: B minor.

CHORALES

The chorale melodies used by the *Lutheran church* were famously harmonized by **Johann Sebastian Bach** (1685-1770) in the mid-18th century and are regarded as a benchmark in classical harmony. As well as being a testimony to Bach's own harmonic virtuosity and sophistication, they demonstrate the extent to which dissonances, unexpected cadences, suspensions, passing notes and sheer harmonic invention can all be contained within the structure of a four-part hymn.

The 371 Chorales, harmonized by J. S. Bach and edited by Albert Riemenschneider are essential study for composers writing in a baroque, classical or romantic style, and are available from all good music shops. Reproduced here is *Es ist genug; so nimm, Herr;* it is one of the most famous chorales and can also be heard at the end of the second movement of the *Violin Concerto* by Alban Berg (1880-1940):

Figure 15-2

Synopsis:

• A full harmonic analysis of the chorale shown here is clearly beyond the scope of this book, though it employs many of the harmonic procedures found in the previous hymn. As with all chorale harmonizations by Bach, it features elaborate modulations, momentary dissonances and passing notes in the inner parts.

Please note the following:

• For the jazz pianist, it is worthwhile playing through any number of hymns and chorales to give us an insight into **four-part harmony** from this period. Furthermore, it will also improve our sight-reading.

• Though the **tenor line** is written in the bass clef, it will often be too high to be played by the left-hand, and will need to be played with the right-hand.

• Hymns and chorales should be played *legato* with an even balance between all four parts, though the soprano line can be given slightly more weight to bring out the melody. This degree of control may be difficult to achieve right away if you have not previously studied classical piano, but playing hymns and chorales on the piano will greatly improve the **sound** you make on the piano.

• Hymns are all written for SATB (soprano, alto, tenor, bass) and sound excellent when sung. Notice that each part is a singable line in accordance with good voice-leading principals.

• It is a worthwhile exercise to analyse a small extract of a hymn or chorale and to then transpose it into other keys, this will help us to **internalise** the harmonic structure.

• Try to **improvise** beyond the extracts chosen by altering the melody, adding rhythmic interest, introducing more suspensions and passing notes etc.

• For an in-depth study of four-part classical harmony, there are many excellent books available. *Harmony* by Walter Piston and *Contrapuntal Technique in the 16th Century* by R. O. Morris are particularly recommended.

THE CLASSICAL PIANO REPERTOIRE

A knowledge of the classical piano repertoire is an invaluable source of information for the jazz pianists. The music composed for piano (or harpsichord) by German or Austrian composers Johann Sebastian Bach (1685-1750), Wolfgang Amadeus Mozart (1756-1791), Ludwig van Beethoven (1770-1821), Franz Schubert (1797-1828), Robert Schumann (1810-1856) and Johannes Brahms (1833-1897); as well as the Italian composer Domenico Scarlatti (1685-1757); the Polish composer Frédéric Chopin (1810-1849); the Russian composers Alexander Skryabin (1872-1915) and Serge Rachmaninov (1873-1943); and the French composers Maurice Ravel (1875-1937), Claude Debussy (1862-1918), Erik Satie (1866-1925) and Olivier Messiaen (1908-1990).

A familiarity with this repertoire is invaluable to any pianist who has not benefited from studying classical piano. After all, it represents centuries of reflection on how to make the piano as an instrument sound best, and we are particularly lucky as pianists to have such a rich musical heritage to draw upon and enjoy.

Though it is clearly beyond the remit of this book to conduct an in-depth study of the influence classical music on jazz piano, certain ideas can be touched upon here, if only to excite a general interest in the music and its relevance to jazz piano. We shall consider the influence of three composers: Ludwig van Beethoven, Frédéric Chopin and Erik Satie.

LUDWIG VAN BEETHOVEN (1770-1827)

Ludwig van Beethoven was himself a virtuoso improviser, and the first major composer to write for the *modern* piano (Mozart's Piano Sonatas were generally conceived for a smaller instrument than the one we know today). The modern piano was developed by Bartolomeo Cristofori in 1709 and used hammers to hit the strings rather than hooks or feathers to pluck the strings, as in a harpsichord. This gave the player greater control over the dynamic range of the piano, which could be controlled by the degree of force exerted on the keyboard. The keyboard was also extended to seven octaves and metal frames were introduced, making it possible to use thicker strings to produce a fuller tone.

Beethoven was quick to embrace these new developments, using the new sonorities for their dramatic and almost orchestral effect, as the opening of the *Pathétique Sonata* demonstrates:

Figure 15-3

Synopsis:

The opening chord of this extract is typical Beethoven, with its stacking of two inversions of a C minor triad in the lower register of the piano for dramatic effect. The first chord is followed by a quieter passage in four parts, the bass moving in contrary motion to the melody in a dotted rhythm. The underlying harmonic progression is Cm to G (dominant) in the first bar; and G (dominant), appearing as diminished seventh chord on A♭, to Cm in the second bar. The use of diminished seventh chords in this way is characteristic of Beethoven.

Beethoven's *Moonlight Sonata* consists entirely of "broken" or "arppegiated" triads in the right-hand, accompanied by octaves in the left-hand:

Figure 15-4

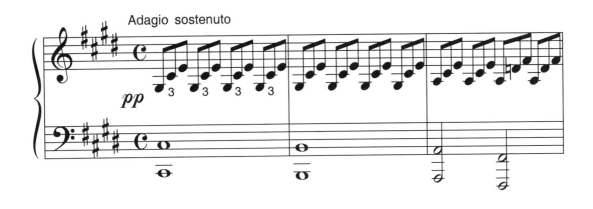

Synopsis:

The harmonic progression of the entire first movement merits further study for its inventive use of modulation and diminished seventh chords. Inversions are used to create a smooth harmonic line in the bass, while triads and seventh chords are played in the right-hand together with a sustained melody note. The use of **octaves** in the left-hand gives the overall chord a deeper sonority, a pianistic device apparent in most of Beethoven's piano music. The playing of triadic structures in the right-hand supported by octaves in the bass is also a feature of many **rock** piano styles.

FREDERIC CHOPIN (1810-1849)

Frédéric Chopin was also a virtuoso pianist and composer who wrote almost exclusively for the piano. His music extended the technical demands on a pianist as well as introducing a more chromatic harmony (ninths, flattened ninths, thirteenths, flattened thirteenths etc.).

Bars 6 to 10 of the *Ballade No. 1 in G Minor* demonstrate Chopin's more chromatic harmony by introducing what jazz theory would term a suspension with a flattened ninth and flattened thirteenth (with no seventh) in bar 2, and a seventh chord with a flattened thirteenth in bar 3:

Figure 15-5

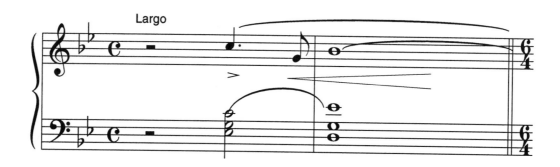

A second feature of Chopin's piano music is the use of **alberti bass**. It consists of chords broken up into patterns played by the left-hand, keeping the music moving while outlining harmonies to support a melody in the right-hand. Mozart used this device extensively to accompany lyrical melodies, though Chopin used it to create a particularly continuous, florid and rhapsodic accompaniment to an intense single line melody. This approach has been taken up by many pianists playing in a "new-age" or "ambient" style.

The opening of Chopin's *Nocturne No. 2, Op. 27,* demonstrates how alberti bass can be used to accompany a single melodic line:

Figure 15-6

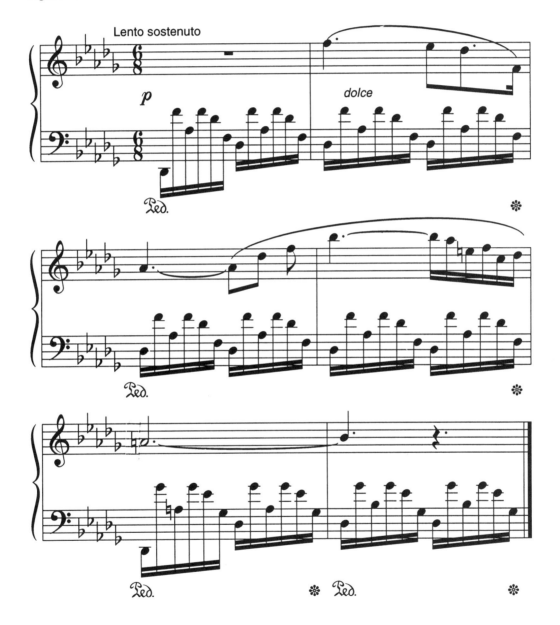

In the opening section of the *Nocturne No. 2, Op. 55,* an alberti bass in appears as a triplet left-hand figure, ascending and descending the arpeggios of each chord in dramatic leaps. In this example, the melodic line takes an almost secondary role to the drama of the left-hand accompaniment:

Figure 15-7

The supreme jazz harmonist Bill Evans incorporated many features of classical piano into his own music, including alberti bass. In the following example, a florid left-hand accompanies a right-hand melody in a II-V-I cadence:

Figure 15-8

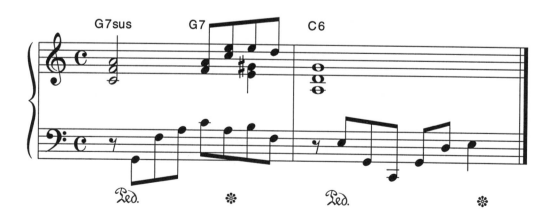

ERIK SATIE (1866-1925)

Jazz harmony has always been heavily influenced by French music - this goes back to the origins of jazz and to the Creole culture in New Orleans in the 1900s that looked to France as its spiritual homeland. The coming together of the Creoles with their allegiance to European musical forms, and the Negroes with their own musical traditions of blues, field hollar, dance and gospel music, were the most formative influences of jazz. The influence of composers from the early 20th century such as Gabriel Fauré, Erik Satie, Claude Debussy and Maurice Ravel, as well as composers of *chansons*, can be clearly heard in the playing of most jazz pianists, in particular Bill Evans, Herbie Hancock, Keith Jarrett and Clare Fischer.

Erik Satie was one of the key conceptualists of the twentieth century whose musical endeavour was to produce a less narrative and more static musical style. The first of his *Three Gynopédies* of 1888 features a "non-developmental" melodic line accompanied by a repetitive or circular modal accompaniment in 3/4 time:

Figure 15-9

This is very reminiscent of Evans' ballad style, when the left-hand would alternate between the bass notes and chords to accompany a florid melodic line:

Figure 15-10

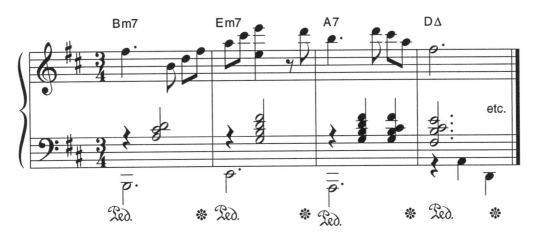

A Classical Approach to Jazz Piano (Harmony) by Dominic Alldis

Apart from the extensive use of seventh chords, a chordal shape introduced as a "partial" voicing in *Chapter Fourteen* is highly suggestive of a French "impressionist" sensibility. Furthermore, the resonance of the following voicing has become almost synonymous with Evans' harmonic concept:

Figure 15-11

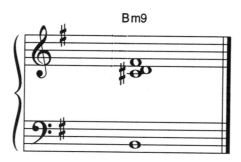

Another feature of Evans' playing is the modal cascading of chords up and down the keyboard. Again, this can be traced back to the influence of French piano music:

Figure 15-12

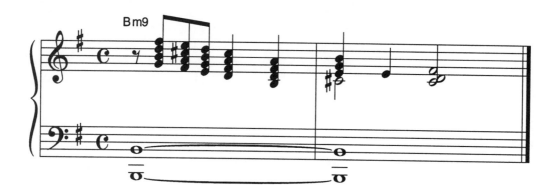

CONCLUSION

Finally, we might mention the harmonic language of the French composer Olivier Messiaen. His "visual" approach to harmony opens up a new world of "sound painting." His pieces for piano, such as *Visions de l'Amen* and *Catalogue d'Oiseaux*, introduce a vast array of densities and textures using both bitonal and modal techniques, combined with dramatic variations in register and dynamics. Several jazz pianists have incorporated these features into their own style, particularly Clare Fischer, Roger Kellaway and Ran Blake.

This chapter represent only a minute insight into classical piano literature - it is intended to engender a general interest in classical piano music from the perspective of a contemporary jazz pianist. As pianists, we are especially lucky to have this rich musical source to draw upon, to engender new music ideas, and inform our improvisational vocabulary.

CONCLUSION

Jazz is an art form that has evolved throughout the century by combining the strengths of many musical idioms. Its melodic and rhythmic origins are mostly from African dance forms and the blues, while its harmonic origins are mostly from European classical harmony. Jazz is also an improvisational language like speech or conversation. The skilled improviser, like the skilled conversationalist, must have access to a musical vocabulary with which to communicate, and the most that any teaching method can do is to present a process that engenders an expansion and development of this musical vocabulary.

Finally, there are no rules in jazz, only questions of musical taste. Nevertheless, a start has to be made, and the process of internalising the harmonic devices shown in this book and studying the musical examples should provide a sound harmonic basis for further study, one that can always be rejected at a later stage. This learning process should be followed by a more open and intuitive approach to learning about the jazz piano idiom - listening to musicians live, transcribing from original recordings, studying written transcriptions of jazz solos, playing and adapting classical and other repertoire, and seeking playing opportunities with other musicians in a wide range of styles.

Good luck and enjoy playing jazz piano!

D.A.

COPYRIGHT ACKNOWLEDGEMENTS